TRENTHAM
REFLECTIONS

GRAHAM BEBBINGTON

Foreword by Mike Herbert

ACKNOWLEDGMENTS

First and foremost, I would like to thank Mike Herbert for writing the foreword to the book.

In addition to those quoted in the text or source notes, I acknowledge most gratefully the assistance of the following:
Philip Bradbeer, Richard A. Durrant, John H. Emery, John Grindey, Mervyn Edwards (Potteries Pub Preservation Society), Peter Davies Dip.TP., MRTPI., John Abberley (The Sentinel), Janet Lee & Julie Taylor (Stoke-on-Trent City Council), Francis Baird (Stafford Borough Council), Gill Mooney (Staffs County Council), Karen Nixon (Trentham Leisure) and Vivien Inge (Birkenhead Land Registry).

Gratitude is also expressed to Mrs D.M.A. Randall, Head of Archives (Staffs County Council), the librarians and staff of Trentham, Hanley, Holmcroft, Newcastle-under-Lyme and Perth & Kinross, and those of the Royal Institute of British Architects and the National Railway Museum.

Finally, my wife Lynne Margaret has, as usual, shared in all the pleasures and pains of research and assisted with everything from IT consultancy to being my soundboard throughout.

Every endeavour has been made to trace source material.
If inadvertently any copyright has been infringed, the author offers his apology and will correct any omission in any subsequent edition.

ALSO BY THE SAME AUTHOR

The Loggerheads Project (Newcastle Borough Council).
Pit Boy to Prime Minister (University of Keele).
A Brief Life (Isle of Wight County Press).
Trentham at War (Churnet Valley Books).
Ship Without Water (Churnet Valley Books).
The Fledglings (Churnet Valley Books).

Cover photo: 'Hot air balloon over lake' *Courtesy of Trentham Leisure*

CHURNET VALLEY BOOKS
1 King Street, Leek, Staffordshire. 01538 399033
www.leekbooks.co.uk
© Graham Bebbington and Churnet Valley Books 2005
ISBN 1 904546 36 6

FOREWORD

Trentham has always been in and out of my life, from my childhood in the 1960s through my school years and one way and another throughout my professional career.

My serious connection started in 1996 when St.Modwen Properties plc purchased the estate and I was given the privilege of leading the team to bring about it's regeneration. I only then began to understand the real significance of Trentham.

The sheer scale of the task we undertook has been daunting but also very exciting and I have learned more than anything just how important Trentham became as an estate of one of Britain's great families. Top architects, landscape designers and great innovators were encouraged to lavish the Sutherland's great wealth at Trentham.

This latest of Graham Bebbington's books brings home a more personal side of Trentham with a collection of stories that connect the famous and not so famous with Trentham and give an insight into the everyday life of a grand estate. The image of Winston Churchill riding on the estate or the lost grandeur of Priory House and the excitement of the many great events in the ballroom, amongst many other stories, conjure up the image that Trentham was always meant to be the centre of attention.

Trentham Reflections is another fascinating insight into Trentham's past and will, I am sure, be a delight to all.

MIKE HERBERT,
Regional Director, St. Modwen Properties plc
Director, Trentham Leisure Ltd.

The South Front, with Grecian Temple.

**"THE GLORY OF TRENTHAM IS THE FRONTING WOOD,
OF AGE AND MAGNIFICENCE"**

5th Viscount Torrington (1743-1813)
from the Torrington Diaries Vol. III Methuen p. 128

CONTENTS

INTRODUCTION

Over the centuries, many have gained pleasure from visiting Trentham in North Staffordshire. Consequently, Trentham means many things to many people whether it be Trentham Gardens, the vast parkland, or the village itself. The new century has heralded the end of one era and the beginning of another, with attention presently focused on the £100m regeneration of the former Sutherland Estate. Trentham is now set to mean much more to even more people. As one person observed - 'it is like a great phoenix rising from the ashes'.

What better time for a fresh look at the history of Trentham? I hope, therefore, that readers may find the following of interest and that in future the material gathered may be considered of sufficient importance to complement that which has already been written.

G.B

May 2005

Trentham's Hollywood-style lido. Photo taken from the Opening Programme, 1936.

BIBLIOGRAPHY

In addition to those works quoted in the source notes, I found the following particularly useful:

The Sentinel Story 1873-1973.

Trentham - a church through history by June Steed (private publication).

History of Trentham & its church from AD 680 by Rev. J.F. Challis (private publication).

The Crusade against Crippledom by Tony Carter (North Staffs Medical Institute).

Millicent, Duchess of Sutherland and the Potteries & Newcastle Cripples' Guild by
D.W. Adams (Staffs County Library).

1. A FRENCH CONNECTION

Children's Cottage and Gardens.

Examination of the Leveson-Gower family history reveals some unusual and fascinating material. For example, one particular incident is reminiscent of a Baroness Orczy plot, as it exposes a link between Lord Granville Leveson-Gower, Marquess of Stafford (1758-1833) and the French Revolution.

The French national holiday commemorates the storming of the Bastille which took place on 14th July 1789. This event marked the beginning of the French Revolution. The Bastille was the notorious state prison and considered to be a token of the absolute and arbitrary power of the King, Louis XVI. To the ordinary rank and file French citizens the storming of the jail was an act of liberty that represented the fight against oppression. It marked the end of absolute monarchy, the birth of the sovereign nation, and subsequently the creation of the first Republic in 1792.

In August 1792, Paris was in turmoil. Crowds had stormed the Tuilleries, the royal palace, and killed several hundred of the Swiss Guard. The King and his Queen, Marie-Antoinette, were forced to flee and take refuge in the Legislative Assembly building where they were placed under house arrest. The violence continued with street fighting and the erection of barricades in various quarters of the city. In the following month the monarchy was officially abolished, and a republic established. Later that year, the King was placed on trial for violating the liberty of his subjects, found guilty and subsequently executed at the guillotine.

Thus the country, and particularly Paris itself, was a dangerous place to be at this time, even more so for foreigners who

Storming the Bastille

were likely to be treated with more suspicion. As it happened, the pottery manufacturer, William Turner of Longton was in the capital on business during this turbulent time. Born in 1762, he was in partnership with his brother at premises in High Street, Lane End. The firm was one of the oldest manufacturers in the trade, having been started by his father (John Turner 1738-1787) who had been appointed potter to the Prince of Wales in 1784. In his contemporary work *History of the Staffordshire Potteries* (1829), Simeon A. Shaw described Turner's company as 'doubtless one of the most experienced in the district.... placed alongside E. Wood and T. Minton'.[1]

Because of the revolution, money was not forthcoming from French debtors. As a consequence, Turner travelled to France to investigate the situation, a decision he was to regret. More or less on arrival, he was arrested on suspicion of being a Dutch spy. A mock tribunal subsequently acquitted him of the charge but nevertheless sentenced him to a period of hard labour. Compelled to work with a pick, he was assigned to work on the demolition of the Bastille. As it happened, the British Ambassador in Paris at the time was none other than Lord Gower, Marquess of Stafford (later 1st Duke of Sutherland). Having been appointed to the post in 1789, he spoke fluent French but, according to Denis Stuart, *'had no other apparent qualities'!* His wife was a friend of Queen Marie-Antoinette, and she sent her clothes during her period of imprisonment. As a result of his appointment, Gower developed a *'taste for things French'*, and his collection included part of the famous 'Queen's necklace'. This was worn in later years by Millicent, Duchess of Sutherland *'with dazzling effect'.*[2]

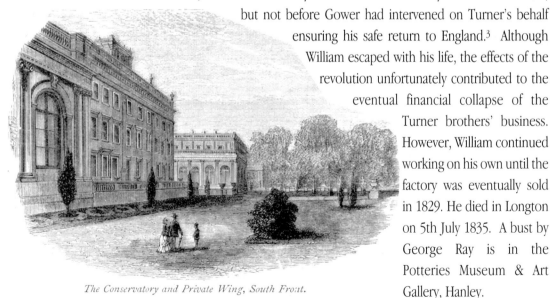

Due to the riotous situation, the British embassy staff had to be hurriedly withdrawn in 1792, but not before Gower had intervened on Turner's behalf ensuring his safe return to England.[3] Although William escaped with his life, the effects of the revolution unfortunately contributed to the eventual financial collapse of the Turner brothers' business. However, William continued working on his own until the factory was eventually sold in 1829. He died in Longton on 5th July 1835. A bust by George Ray is in the Potteries Museum & Art Gallery, Hanley.

The Conservatory and Private Wing, South Front.

NOTES
1. Reprinted by S.R Publishers (1970) pp75/76.
2. Denis Stuart, *Dear Duchess* (Victor Gollancz)(1982) p31.
3. *Staffordshire Advertiser* 11th July 1835.

2. A MONUMENTAL JOURNEY

Centuries ago, with the absence of a public transport system, and only the rich able to afford a horse, skilled craftsmen tended to walk to a new place of employment, having completed a contract or assignment. This may have involved relocating from one area of the country to another and even in the period that Britain formed part of the Roman Empire, this was not unusual. For example, whilst the construction of Hadrian's Wall, the length of which runs from Wallsend-on-Tyne to Bowness-on- Solway, was commenced by Roman soldiers around AD120, historians tell us that sections of it were actually completed by craftsmen from the south west of England! Nonetheless, it may be surprising for some to learn that a Hanford firm owes its origins to someone who in the 19th Century walked some 300 miles to gain employment at Trentham with George Granville Leveson-Gower, the 2nd Duke of Sutherland (1786-1861).

The Duke had married Harriet, a daughter of the 6th Earl of Carlisle, who proved to be an exciting, energetic and enterprising lady, if not an expensive choice! Between eleven pregnancies, she encouraged her husband to rebuild or improve a number of the family properties. In the 1820s Lilleshall Hall, their Shropshire seat, was rebuilt, and major improvements also made to Stafford House (now Lancaster House), in London. Subsequently, between the years 1834-1844, they rebuilt Trentham Hall to the Italianate design of Sir Charles Barry at a cost exceeding £260,000. The services of the landscape wizard Lancelot 'Capability' Brown (1715-1783) had been employed to enhance the parkland of the earlier house and this, together with Barry's new Italian 'palazzo' and garden, provided a setting which enraptured the many guests and visitors who came to the estate. The sight is said to have prompted Benjamin Disraeli in the opening of his novel Lothair to write *'it would be difficult to find a fairer scene than Brentham'* (Trentham).

The rebuilding of Trentham Hall resulted in an additional demand for the services of certain craftsmen, particularly stone masons, and whilst on business in Scotland, the Duke let it be known that there was work available for such trade on his North Staffordshire estate. Among those hearing news of the Trentham vacancies was 19 year old Robert Burt. Born at Kelty in the Parish of Cleish on 18th November 1816, he was the son of Robert and Martha Burt (nee Hepburn). His father was a factor (estate manager) at 'Blairadam,' Maryburgh - the family home of the Adam architectural dynasty. As factor, he would have been on good terms with the estate owners, and the biographical dictionary of Kinross-shire, *Distinguished Men of the County,* contains reference to Robert Burt as *'being on terms of intimate friendship with the Adam family.'*

According to his great, great grandson Wilf Burt, Robert Burt Jnr was a time-served mason and is understood to have been working on a cathedral or church in the Kinross area at the time. It is also known that major repair and improvement works were in progress at 'Blairadam' and he could have been employed there, particularly in view of the family connection. Whatever his situation, it is believed that the contract was nearing completion, as a consequence of which Robert Burt Jnr and a colleague decided to take their chances and undertake the long journey to North Staffordshire.

The two men eventually made their way south following a route which took them through the Lake District. However, it was here that for some reason Robert's companion decided to return home, leaving him to complete the 300 mile journey on foot on his own. It is believed that the trek took approximately one month, walking during daylight hours and then spending the night in various houses and establishments en route.

On arrival in 1836, he was employed on the rebuilding of Trentham Hall and he found lodgings in nearby Hanford where four years later he married local girl Lucy Knapper. The couple went on to have eight children. In 1840 with work at the Hall for the stone masons coming to an end, Robert decided to set up his own business. This was operated from the yard at the rear of his Hanford home, the site of which is now occupied by the Staffordshire Knot public house. Initially, he carried out various tasks such as general masonry work, building fireplaces, repairs to churches, and building and repairing walls. Eventually, however, he decided to concentrate on memorial and monumental work, and his six sons joined him in succession in the business.

Thus the monumental firm of Burts became firmly established, subsequently moving to its present premises in Wilson Road in 1937. In addition to serving the community, the Burt family have also continued to serve the Sutherland family. Over the years Wilf and his late father have repaired the family's monuments at Tittensor church, the base of Chantrey's colossal bronze statue of the 1st Duke which dominates the hill overlooking the southern end of the lake, and also the extensive boundary wall which abuts Eccleshall Road to the rear of the Trentham Estate. All because of an enterprising young man who walked 300 miles for a job!

Wilf Burt and his son working on the Queen Victoria statue,
Newcastle-under-Lyme, July 2001.

3. DEVEY - THE FORGOTTEN ARCHITECT

When considering the history of Trentham in relation to its architecture, the names of Sir Charles Barry and Charles Heathcote Tatham are quintessential. The name of the Victorian architect George Devey is rarely if ever mentioned and yet he made a number of contributions to Trentham and the other estates owned by the Sutherland family.

The son of a solicitor, Devey was born in London on 23rd February 1820. After attending Kings College School he became a pupil architect and surveyor at the busy practice of Thomas Little off Trafalgar Square. Devey had a talent for watercolours, possessing 'a painter's eye' and the ability to capture the mood of a place, and it is believed that this led him to seek a career in architecture. In 1846 he set off on a continental tour with a colleague, Coutts Stone, who became a life-long friend. A number of sketches and watercolours undertaken by both men during the tour have survived, and the influence on Devey's future use of building methods and materials is evident.

On his return to England he sought to gain his own commissions. Devey's career was slow to take off until he was introduced in 1848 to the wealthy Kent landowners Lord De L'Isle of Penshurst Place, and Lt. General Sir Henry Hardinge (a former Governor-General of India), owner of South Park, Penshurst. Both employed him, first, Lord De L'Isle, on the restoration of and additions to a group of cottages named Leicester Square, situated near to Penshurst Church. This scheme was so successful that Devey was employed on the estate until the mid 1870s restoring not only Penshurst Place itself, but also carrying out improvements to the village and estate cottages.

His work for Hardinge included the enlargement of the buildings at South Park Home Farm and it was here, and at Leicester Square, according to Dr Jill Allibone, where he *first employed the style and materials based on the vernacular buildings of the Weald.* This enabled him to *formulate a style of building which was to characterise his own work* and which had *'a demonstrable effect on the younger architects.'*[1]

Satisfied clients recommended George Devey to others and eventually Lord De L'Isle introduced him to the 2nd Duke of Sutherland whose wife Harriett was Mistress of the Robes to Queen Victoria. A former pupil was later to observe that the introduction was *'...the first step on the ladder after which he rapidly rose to the summit.'*[2] The Duke had three other principal country estates in addition to Trentham, at Cliveden in Buckinghamshire, Dunrobin Castle in Sutherland and Lilleshall in Shropshire. After working initially at Cliveden, Devey was employed on them all.

On the Trentham estate his work was generally confined to cottages and farmhouses in the Wealden style. Although many of Devey's drawings and plans have survived and may be seen at the Staffordshire Record Office and the Royal Institute of British Architects' Library, some do not precisely identify their location on the Trentham estate. However, existing examples are Gravel Pit Lodge on the Eccleshall Road, Toft Farm, and the former Tittensor village school (now part of Bassett's Transport). The latter was the first of many schools built for landowners.

George Devey
Courtesy of RIBA

Gravel Pit Lodge, Trentham Park.

Also in Staffordshire, Devey was employed by the Bass family at Rangemore and by Lord Bagot on his Blithfield estate. Future commissions included work for the likes of the 5th Earl Spencer on his Northamptonshire estate, the 6th Baron Vernon at Sudbury, and various members of the de Rothschild family. Many outstanding examples of Devey's work survive in London in particular Lennox Gardens, Grosvenor Gardens and Cadogan Square. His greatest monument is possibly Ascott House in Buckinghamshire, the former residence of Leopold de Rothschild.

Devey's practice was in Great Marlborough Street, London until 1880 when he relocated to 123 Bond Street, a more prestigious address. He never married, and lived with his parents until they died. Devey was a man capable of working on more than one project at a time, but eventually the constant visiting of work in progress took its toll, and following a site inspection in Ireland he developed pneumonia and died at Hastings on 4th November 1886 at the age of 66. Subsequently, Percy G. Stone (son of Coutts Stone mentioned earlier) spoke of the *'marvellous sketches'* made by his former master, and testified to his *'extremely sensitive and kindly nature'*, exercising *'old fashioned courtesy to whoever he met, whether in business or society.'*[3]

Devey's practice appears to have been very prosperous but his clients were mainly drawn from the upper classes who did not particularly care for their business to be a matter for public discussion. Therefore, Devey did not perhaps receive the attention he otherwise might have done, and sadly his name has rather passed into obscurity. But Devey was appreciated by fellow architects and his use of the vernacular was widely adopted by the next generation, becoming the basis for the design of the traditional country house. His style was the forerunner of the arts and crafts school of design developed by architects such as Voysey and Edwin Lutyens.

NOTES
1. Jill Allibone, *George Devey.* The Lutterworth Press (1991) p23
2. RIBA Journal of Proceedings 18th November 1886 pp 46-47.
3. Ibid

4. 'THESPIS' & THE LEVESON-GOWER CONNECTION

Sir William Schwenck (W.S.) Gilbert (1836-1911) was possibly the most brilliant dramatist of Victorian England. A daring and cynical playwright, he was also a prolific journalist and humorous poet. He achieved worldwide fame through his collaboration with Sir Arthur Sullivan (1842-1900) creating such classics as *The Mikado, Iolanthe,* and the other ever popular 'Savoy Operas.' Gilbert's eye for detail and his satirical mill resulted in superb librettos which, together with Sullivan's delightful scores, ensured their lasting popularity. At the time that they were written people knew where they stood in society, and if they forgot - as writer Michael Ffinch observed - *'Gilbert soon reminded them of it!'*[1]

He invited them to share his sense of fun and, in a way, laugh at themselves and the absurdity of situations, particularly in the political arena. Gilbert's satirising of certain well known contemporary personalities, such as W.H. Smith (*HMS Pinafore*)

Sullivan   Gilbert

and Captain B.M. Shaw (*Iolanthe*), are well documented, but it is not generally appreciated that the libretto of *Thespis* includes a gentle satire aimed at George Granville William Leveson-Gower, the 3rd Duke of Sutherland (1828-1892). Act 1 of the opera features the so called 'Junction Song' which H.M. Wallbrook in 1922 described as *'a genial quizzing of the Duke'* in his work *Gilbert and Sullivan - a history and comment.*[2]

The Sutherland title was the Senior Scottish earldom and the family was immensely rich. The Duke had a number of properties including Dunrobin, in Sutherland, Trentham Hall, Lilleshall, and Stafford House, London (now Lancaster House) together with 1.5 million acres of land which in 1883 yielded £141,000 pa.[3]

According to his grandson, the Duke was particularly venturesome having spent a fortune developing the County of Sutherland by providing infrastructure and improving land for agricultural purposes. An owner of a

Dunrobin Castle, the main residence of the Dukes of Sutherland in Scotland, where they held massive estates.

number of colleries, he was also renowned for his interest in railways, having an insatiable passion for driving engines.[4] In 1870, when the railway had been constructed as far as Golspie (2 miles south of the Dunrobin Estate) he extended the line by 17 miles to Helmsdale at his own expense, to serve both his castle and the fishing villages on the coast. Anxious to provide a public service as soon as practicable, he not only built stations on the length of private line, but also acquired an engine and rolling stock. The Duke's engine was a 21 ton 2-4-0 tank type, designed and built by Kitson of Leeds and proudly bore the name 'Dunrobin'.[5] It is also interesting to note that the private railway remained with the family until nationalisation in 1950.[6]

Courtesy Elizabeth, Countess of Sutherland

George Granville William Leveson-Gower, 3rd Duke of Sutherland in the uniform of the 93rd Highlanders.

The Duke was said to be of a *'carefree, independent nature, not always particular about etiquette.'* He is also said to have been responsible for popularising the smoking of cigarettes, flaunting the taboo which did not allow smoking in public places at the time.[7] When he died in 1892, The Times printed an obituary notice containing the following characteristic anecdote: *'an admiring navvy seeing him start from Dunrobin Station one day explained to his mate - 'there! that's what I call a real dook! Look at him a-driving of 'is own engine, on 'is own railway, an' burnin' 'is own blessed coal!'*[8] It is that free and easy attitude that made him very popular in some quarters, and which possibly drew him to the attention of Gilbert, assuming that he did not know him anyway.

Thespis or 'The Gods Grown Old' was the first Gilbert and Sullivan collaboration and their sole purpose-written Christmas entertainment. According to Gilbert's biographer Jane W. Stedman, the plot gave *'a new twist to old patterns of burlesquing the classics.'*[9] Thespis and his company of Thessalonian actors picnic on Mount Olympus where the gods have become elderly and incapable of fulfilling their divine functions. Actors and gods change places, the latter going to earth for a year, the former taking their nominal identities, while Mercury the only young god stays on to assist them.

With Sullivan's brother Frederick playing Apollo, *Thespis* was first staged on Boxing Day 1871 at the Gaiety Theatre, London. The title role was taken by John Lawrence Toole, a recently joined member of the Gaiety company, but who nevertheless had earlier found fame as Bob Crachit in an adaptation of Dicken's *A Christmas Carol*. Gilbert gave *Thespis* the following song about the railway (ie. the 'Junction Song') which was a precursor of his later patter songs, and it is this which is said to be 'a general quizzing' of the Duke of Sutherland:

> 'I once knew a chap who discharged a function
> On the North South East West Diddlesex Junction.
> He was conspicuous exceeding,
> For his affable ways, and his easy breeding.
> Although a chairman of directors,
> He was hand in glove with the ticket inspectors.
> He tipped the guards with brand new fivers,
> And sang little songs to the engine drivers.

Chorus 'Twas told to me with great compunction,
By one who had discharged with unction
A chairman of directors function
On the North South East West Diddlesex Junction.
Fol diddle, lol diddle, lol lol lay.

Each Christmas Day he gave each stoker
A silver shovel and a golden poker.
He'd buttonhole flowers for the ticket sorters
And rich Bath-buns for the outside porters.
He'd mount the clerks on his first-class hunters,
And he built little villas for the road-side shunters,
And if any were fond of pigeon shooting,
He'd ask them down to his place at Tooting.
Chorus 'Twas told to me...etc.

In course of time there spread a rumour
That he did all of this from a sense of humour.
So instead of signalling and stoking,
they gave themselves up tp a course of joking.
Whenever they knew that he was riding,
They shunted his train on a lonely siding,
Or stopped all night in the middle of a tunnel,
On the plea that the boiler was a-coming through the funnel
Chorus

If he wished to go to Perth or Sterling,
His train through several counties whirling,
Would set him down in a fit of larking,
At four a.m in the wilds of Barking.
This pleased his whim and seemed to strike it,
But the general public did not like it.
The receipts fell, after a few repeatings,
and he got it hot at the annual meetings.
Chorus

He followed out his whim with vigour,
The shares went down to a nominal figure.
These are the sad results proceeding,
From his affable ways and his easy breeding,
The line, with its rails and guards and peelers,
Was sold for a song to marine store dealers
The shareholders are all in the work'us,
And he sells pipe-lights in the Regent Circus.
Chorus

The performance of the song was said to have *'brought the house down'* with the Pall Mall Gazette also commenting that *'the orchestration is very novel including as it does, the employment of a railway bell, a railway whistle and some new instrument of music imitating the agreeable sound of a train in motion.'*[10]

In addition, the critic of the Sunday Times described the song as '*the hit of the night... the entire company joining in the chorus, the music of which admirably expresses the whirl and thunder of a railway train at express speed.*'[11] Whilst basking in the success of his first oratorio *The Prodigal Son* and the operatic venture *Cox*

Courtesy Elizabeth, Countess of Sutherland

The grand opening of the Duke of Sutherland's railway between Golspie and Helmsdale, by Princess Christian, October 1870.

and Box, Sullivan was nonetheless disappointed with *Thespis,* being of the opinion that few of the cast could actually sing. But even if he held such a view, his admiration for Gilbert as a producer was firmly established. Sullivan had noticed how strict Gilbert could be as he rehearsed and drilled the chorus, and his ability to keep the upper hand with the principals. It was also on attending a performance of *Thespis* that Richard D'Oyly Carte is believed to have first seen the potential of Gilbert and Sullivan, and which ultimately lead to their long and successful association.[12]

Thespis enjoyed only a modest success, finishing its run after 64 performances. Also, whilst Gilbert's libretto has survived, this was not published until 1911, the last year of his life.[13] In addition, the score has not survived, although the ballet music was rediscovered in 1989. Apparently dissatisfied with his music, Sullivan is understood to have gone to great lengths to retrieve all copies, no doubt to destroy them. As a result, although the opera has been revived on occasion, it features a score adapted from Sullivan's other music or pastiche. The circumstances being as they were ie a modest run and the score not surviving has meant that *Thespis* is rarely performed and it is no doubt for this reason that the connection with the Duke of Sutherland has been lost sight of.

NOTES
1. Michael Ffinch, *Gilbert & Sullivan* (Weidenfeld & Nicholson) p. 12
2. See also Ibid p45, and John Van Der Kiste, *Gilbert & Sullivan's Christmas* (Sutton Publishing) p25
3. Denis Stuart, *Dear Duchess* (Victor Gollancz) p30
4. The 5th Duke of Sutherland, *Looking Back* (Odhams) p33
5. J.R.H. Cormack & J.L. Stevenson, *Highland Railway Locomotives Book 1* (The Railway Correspondence & Travel Soc.) p137
6. Brian Masters, *The Dukes* (Blond & Briggs) p336
7. Ibid p336
8. Terence Rees, *Thespis - a Gilbert & Sullivan Enigma* p39
9. Jane W. Stedman, *W.S. Gilbert* (OUP) p95
10. Pall Mall Gazette 3 January 1872
11. Sunday Times, 31 December 1871
12. Michael Ffinch, op. cit p55
13. Terence Rees, op. cit p90

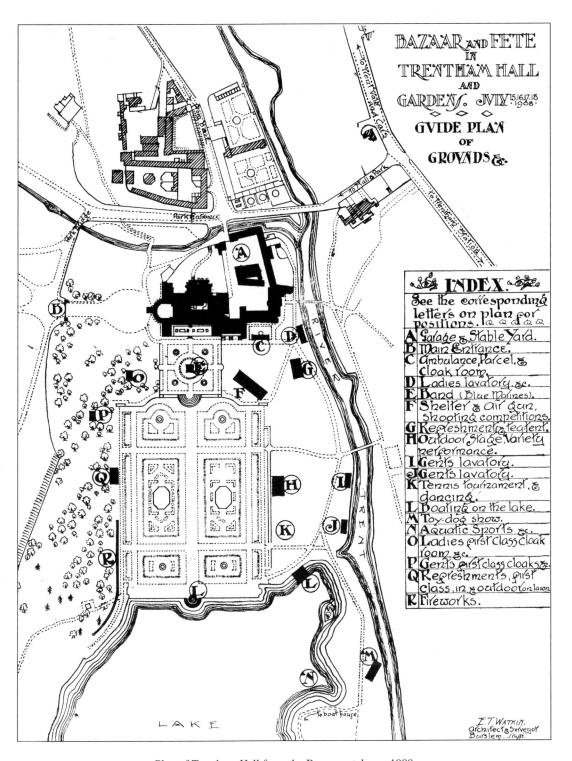

Plan of Trentham Hall from the Bazaar catalogue 1908.

Horse team and hay cart on the Trentham estate weighbridge by Peacock Cottages. Thomas Furnival (2nd huntsman to the Duke of Sutherland) is seen on the passenger seat. *Bebbington collection.*

Ash Green, early 20th century. *Courtesy Mrs Barbara Hobson*

5. WINSTON'S DEBT

Thomas Furnival and his family resided at Crown Cottage on the west side of the A34 Stone Road at Trentham. The property no longer exists, but was situated between Cranberry Cottage and the junction with Whitmore Road (or Dog Kennel Lane as it was then known). Being also positioned opposite the North Staffs Hunt Stables (the former Trentham Inn) the cottage was ideally located, as Tom held the position of 2nd Huntsman to Cromartie, the 4th Duke of Sutherland (1852-1913) - His Grace being No.1!

Since 1862 the hunt stables had been managed at Trentham, its employees being maintained at the Sutherland's expense. The Duke and his wife Millicent shared one particular interest, that of hunting, and their life was said to have hinged around the sporting calendar. The couple hunted regularly and she had six horses for her own riding.[1] Up to 60 hunters were stabled at Trentham, and a pack of 50-60 hounds were kennelled nearby in premises off aptly named Dog Kennel Lane. On occasions when the hunt was meeting, Tom Furnival would be easily identifiable as No.2 Huntsman, dressed in black, as opposed to the familiar red of the other riders.

Born at Hodnet in 1866, Tom is believed to have accompanied the Duke to Trentham upon his succession to the title, having been previously employed on the family's estate at Lilleshall. *'Small in stature, built like a jockey with twinkling blue eyes'* he was, according to his grand-daughter Mrs Thelma Shanahan, *'much loved and a real character with always a tale to tell'.* A popular and highly respected employee on the Trentham Estate, Tom Furnival was also renowned for the pearls of wisdom which he regularly imparted to friends, relatives and colleagues alike, an example being *'you can always tell a man by his shoes!'*

At Crown Cottage, Tom and his wife Elizabeth were blessed with 4 children. The family home was similar in appearance to the surviving Cranberry Cottage, with shuttered windows. Access was via three steps, down from pavement level to the front door. The ground floor accommodation consisted of a large front room (which regularly served as the local polling station) and kitchen, with two bedrooms above. There was also a very useful large cellar below stairs. Although one might not perhaps describe Crown Cottage as grandly furnished, the Furnivals nevertheless possessed some impressive pieces of furniture, including a fine antique table which had

Tom and Elizabeth Furnival.
Courtesy Mrs T. Shanahan

The four Furnival children,
L to R, Hilda, Phyllis,
Arthur and Doris. c.1907.
Courtesy Mrs T. Shanahan

Mr and Mrs Salmon taken in
1928 when Mr Salmon was 90
He was the last coachman
whilst the Duke of Sutherland
resided at Trentham.
Mrs Salmon was renowned for
her dripping cake.
Courtesy Vera Hicks

been presented to them by the Duke. Outside facilities included a two seater toilet and pig sty. According to Mrs Shanahan, her grandfather regularly killed pigs, and black pudding was a family speciality.

Being employed on the estate in the position that he was, Tom Furnival was an authority on horses. Renowned for his handling skills, he was often seen in the estate's smithy, shoeing horses himself. His expertise was put to greater use during World War I when, together with his son Arthur, he broke in animals for the Army Remount Depot at nearby Butterton.[2] The Remount Service provided 1.5 million horses and mules during the course of the Great War, being used for various purposes eg officers' mounts, cavalry, hauling guns and stores etc. The service reached its peak during the war period. Thereafter its size and role declined as mechanisation increased.

Winston Leonard Spencer Churchill (later Sir 1874-1965) was a friend and frequent guest of the Sutherlands. He too was a fine horseman and whilst serving in India as a young officer, he discovered that the most serious business of life in the army there was polo. His regiment won the All-India Cavalry Cup and Churchill himself was in the team in spite of the handicap of an injured shoulder.[3] Churchill's first appearance in the House of Commons was in February 1901, and it was around that period that he stayed at Trentham for a short visit. However, on his arrival on the Friday he soon learned that the Duke unexpectedly had to leave for London on urgent business the following morning.

Nonetheless, His Grace made arrangements for Churchill to be entertained in his absence, including a ride. Tom Furnival was instructed to prepare horses and accompany the young politician, and together they rode over the rolling countryside to Woore, there being little but fields en route at the time. On their return to the hall, Winston dismounted, shook hands with Tom, commented on how much he had enjoyed the day out, and expressed what pleasure it had been to ride with him. Before returning the horses to the stables, Churchill remarked that he didn't carry money with him but that on his return to London, he would send Tom a gold sovereign at his first opportunity. To be promised such an amount would, at the time, have been regarded by someone in Tom's position as most generous - naturally he was said to have been *very pleased*. However, the promise was never fulfilled. Afterwards Tom frequently commented that Winston Churchill owed him a sovereign!

Another regular duty of the 2nd Huntsman was to attend Duchess Millicent on her rides at Trentham. According to biographer Denis Stuart *'he was often hard pressed to keep up. She rode well up with the hounds, despite the occasional fall and the dangers from wire fencing put in hedges by some of the more unsportsmanlike farmers.'* *'Riding was her favourite pastime, even if* *it was not an all consuming passion'* he also wrote. The Duchess rode every day after breakfast, having taken morning prayers with the assembled domestic staff clad in her riding habit.[4]

With the advent of the motor car, both the Duke and Duchess became keen drivers. In fact, the Duchess was the first President of the Ladies Automobile Club. However, when the Duke acquired his first vehicle, which he referred to as *'The Thing',* he instructed Tom Furnival to ride on horseback in front of the limousine as a safety measure during its first outing at Trentham. According to Thelma Shanahan, they set off along Longton Road until they reached the Trentham Hotel. Here Tom found himself unable to prevent the horse turning into the hotel grounds, and the animal stopped at the entrance where it refused to move. The Duke followed, and on alighting from the vehicle quipped *'Right Tom, I now know where you spend your lunchtimes!'*

On another occasion the Duke and Duchess visited nearby Maer Hall, home of the Harrison family. Tom and a number of the domestic staff accompanied them. *'It was like an episode from* *the popular television series Upstairs, Downstairs'* observed Thelma. She recalled how her grandfather saved the day after the cooks burnt the stew and didn't know how to retrieve the situation. Tom suggested putting jam into the pot, whereupon they looked at him in surprise. *'Just* *do it'* he said. Accordingly, a small amount of jam was poured into the pot and duly stirred. When it was eventually served, there was no comment from upstairs!

Passionate about cricket, Tom Furnival played regularly as wicket keeper in the local team and also maintained the pitch. Another passion was playing cards. He was said to be an expert at cribbage. On his retirement he continued to work on a part-time basis but also loved to rummage in the estate's refuse yard behind Cranberry Cottage from where he rescued many 'treasures.' Accompanied by his grand-daughter, this was a favourite pastime. Although not a drinker as such, he liked to visit the old Staffordshire Knot at Hanford each evening, walking along the main road from his cottage. Here he regularly purchased two bottles of Double Diamond for home consumption. In the meantime, his wife would have the poker in the fire to enable it to be inserted into their drinks on his return.

Tom died in 1954 and was laid to rest at Trentham near to where he lived and tended to his beloved horses. According to the family, his death resulted from a broken heart, having lost his wife one year earlier.

NOTES

1. Denis Stuart, *Dear Duchess* (Victor Gollancz) p39
2. Although little is know about the Butterton Depot, records indicate that it came under Northern Command and one of a number which relied heavily on civilian assistance. PRO Ref: WO107/26
3. Malcolm Thomson, *Churchill, his life and times* (Odhams) p8
4. Denis Stuart, op.cit

6. THE PEN OF MILLICENT, DUCHESS OF SUTHERLAND

Millicent, Duchess of Sutherland (1867-1955) was, as her obituary in the Manchester Guardian states, *'a remarkable woman'.* Noted society beauty and diplomatic hostess of the Victorian and Edwardian eras, she became a legend in her own lifetime. Described as *'a latter day Helen of Troy'* by Winston Churchill, who knew her well, she enjoyed the fame that her beauty, wealth and title brought.

Nevertheless, from an early age she also shared a deep concern for the quality of life of those less fortunate, particularly children, although, in performing some excellent work in this field she was, on occasion misunderstood, criticised and ridiculed. For example, her successful campaign on behalf of pottery workers to ban the use of lead-based glazes, the cause of much chronic poisoning, actually resulted in some manufacturers, who resented her interference, branding her as *'Meddlesome Millie'.* As some readers will be aware, this did not go unnoticed by Hanley born novelist Arnold Bennett (1867-1931) who caricatured her as the 'Countess of Chell' in his *Tales of the Five Towns* and *The Card.* Paraphrasing her local nickname as 'Interfering Iris' in *The Burglary (The Grim Smile of the Five Towns)*, he describes the Countess as *'pretty'* and exercising from Sneyd Hall that *'condescending meddlesomeness which so frequently exasperates the Five Towns'.*

Although she inspired Bennett and was immortalised by him, it is not generally appreciated that the Duchess herself possessed literary skills. She wrote poetry for much of her adult life and had some of it published, together with several books and numerous articles. She cultivated the literary set and several, including J.M. Barrie, were frequently invited to the family seats at Trentham and Dunrobin.

Her earliest book was entitled *How I Spent My Twentieth Year.* Published in 1889, it was based on a diary of a round-the-world trip she undertook with her husband, intended to aid recuperation following the difficult birth of her first child. A novel, *One Hour and the Next*, dealing with working class life, followed in 1899. Whereas the Manchester Guardian described the work as *'having no striking merit'*, the critic nevertheless went on to say that the book was *'smoothly written and for one in her position, it showed some power of entering into the life of a class far removed from her own'.*

Her attack on the use of lead in the pottery industry was published in 1901 as a chapter in a book on the history of working conditions in the potbanks (*'On the dangerous processes in the potting industry'* in *The Staffordshire Potter* by H. Owen). The following year saw publication of *The Winds of the World.* Drawing on her extensive travels to provide authentic detail, the book consisted of a collection of short stories on the theme of love set in different parts of the world.

Subsequently, she became involved in a project of a different nature compiling an anthology of the work of living poets. Under the title of *The Wayfarer's Love*, the book published in 1904, consisted of contributions specially written for the collection. The impressive list of contributors included A.E. Housman, W.B. Yeats, G.K. Chesterton, and John Masefield. All profits from sales went to the Potteries & Newcastle Cripples' Guild which she had established in 1900.

Stafford House – Exterior.

Stafford House – State Drawing Room.

Trentham Hall.

Lilleshall House.

Some of the homes of the Duke and Duchess of Sutherland, from the Bazaar catalogue 1908.
They were amongst the richest people in Britain.

Millicent herself wrote poetry during this period, some of which was published in the Westminster Gazette. She also attempted a new literary form, a play in blank verse entitled *The Conquerer*. Having written this under the pseudonym of R.E. Fyffe, she submitted a draft to the famous actor/manager Sir Johnston Forbes-Robertson who selected it for the opening production at London's Scala Theatre on 23rd September 1905. Millicent was delighted, believing that she had achieved a breakthrough into the world of literature by her own talent, since she revealed her identity only when permission was sought to modify the script.

Forbes-Robertson persuaded Edward German to compose the incidental music to the play which was seen as a shrewd move. The two men had worked together before and German was then at the height of his fame following the success of his operetta *Merrie England* some three years earlier. *The Conquerer* was a blood-thirsty tale of Morven, a warlord, who rampaged across the nations in his quest for global domination. According to Tim McDonald, whose notes accompany the recordings of German's music, the play was *'all good solid, overheated, macho nonsense'* but *'a rather surprising product for a lady of the nobility.'* Sadly, as happens sometimes today, the production was not a success and it closed after twelve performances.

In the 1914-18 War, Millicent was among the first of a number of titled ladies to establish an overseas hospital under the auspices of the Red Cross. The Millicent Sutherland Ambulance, as the unit became known, was quickly caught up in hostilities when Germany invaded Belgium but fortunately was given authority to leave occupied territory. On her return to England, having seen the need, Millicent began to organise a new unit to transport wounded soldiers. To fund this she wrote an account of her experiences entitled *Six Weeks at the War* which was published in The Times. With the aid of Winston Churchill, then First Lord of the Admiralty, she returned to France with her new unit comprising doctors, nurses, drivers, and eight cars. Her subsequent experiences and her anguish at witnessing the daily tragedies of young servicemen dying in torment are reflected in the following lines written after the death of one particular young French soldier:

> 'He was so young to die;
> Ah! these are catchwords now
> When Death sucks red lips white
> Yet laurel crowns the brow.
>
> Why did we wish him life?
> Why did we feel a pang?
> The while we slaked his thirst
> And round us night flies sang.
>
> He lived from night to dawn
> And all the hot day through
> While fever lit his eyes
> His limbs no resting knew.

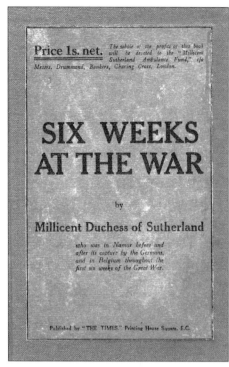

The cover of Millicent's book about the medical team she led to Belgium at the beginning of the 1st World War.

The cover of the official catalogue for the Bazaar and Fair that Millicent organised at Trentham for the Potteries Cripples' Guild and the Duchess of Sutherland's School for Cripples.

Millcent with her team of nurses in Belgium at the beginning of the 1st World War.

And with the setting sun
Outward his spirit leapt -
In calm the moon arose
Only the sister wept.'

Reproduced by kind permission of Elizabeth, Countess of Sutherland

In addition to her ambulance work, Millicent established a hospital on the outskirts of Dunkirk, which by the time of the Somme offensive had become part of the British army's medical services. It received its share of the 20,000 casualties from the first day's fighting and went on to perform valuable service throughout the war. Later, 'Sister Millicent' (as she became known by patients and staff) was awarded the British Royal Red Cross for her services. In addition she received the Belgian equivalent and the French honoured her with the Croix de Guerre and the Medaille des Epidemies.

After the war Millicent spent most of her life in France, continuing to write for newspaper and magazines. Her last major publication was the semi-autobiographical *That Fool of a Woman* published in 1925. She is known to have been working on a play in 1929 but the text is not thought to have survived. Millicent died at her home in Orriule on 20th August 1955. Following cremation, her ashes were buried at the private family cemetery at Dunrobin, Scotland.

Millicent, Duchess of Sutherland, with her daughter,
Lady Rosemary Leveson-Gower.

THE POTTERIES CRIPPLES' GUILD was established some eight years ago for the relief and assistance of Crippled Children amongst the poorer classes in the Pottery towns. To-day this Guild has the names of nearly 400 children on its books, and is divided into three divisions, all of which merit the attention and interest of the public.

Firstly, there is the Convalescent Home at Woore, where sometimes for months spinal cases, hip cases and deformities of other kinds are treated, and the children, by good food and by healthy air and happy surroundings, are restored to a large measure of activity, and indeed, save in exceptional cases, to complete health.

The nine beds in this Home are filled by boys and girls sent from various districts in North Staffordshire, not always from the Pottery towns, although preference is given when possible to children from these towns. It is hoped, if more money is forthcoming, to increase the number of beds to eleven.

Secondly, there are Voluntary Committees in the towns of Hanley, Stoke, Longton, Fenton, Burslem and Tunstall. The ladies who belong divide amongst themselves the onerous duties of visiting the Cripples in their districts; they become friends of the children, and report on their wants to the General Secretary or to the Honorary Medical Officer. Nourishing food is given at discretion, and a successful endeavour has been made to teach those crippled children who are fairly active the rudiments of needlework and other light forms of employment in Spare-Time Classes.

The ladies on these Committees are really carrying on a labour of love, and money is urgently needed by them to supply surgical instruments to the children under their charge, and to give them an oft-needed change at the seaside or in the country, for it may well be understood that the Woore Home with only nine beds cannot receive them all.

SPECIAL TRAIN
ARRANGEMENTS.

The LONDON AND NORTH-WESTERN, MIDLAND, GREAT WESTERN and GREAT NORTHERN RAILWAY COMPANIES will issue Cheap Tickets at a fare-and-a-quarter to Trentham, from all Stations within a radius of 60 miles. The Tickets will be issued upon each day of the Fête by any train leaving before mid-day, and they will be available for the return journey by any train having a through connection on the day of issue only.

The NORTH STAFFORDSHIRE RAILWAY COMPANY will issue Cheap Tickets from all their Stations to Trentham upon each day of the Fête. For full particulars see the Company's Special Bills.

Motor Cars, 'Buses, and other Conveyances, will run between Trentham Station, the Tram Terminus and the Hall, at a charge not exceeding 2d.

Two interesting cuttings from Bazaar catalogue in 1908.

7. JAMES HICKS - THE LAST GAMEKEEPER

There is an old country saying that *'gamekeepers are born and not made'* and in this a certain amount of truth still remains. The basic qualities required were loyalty, a genuine concern for fellow men, and a detailed knowledge and love of the countryside and natural history. Commitment to the job was total - 365 days a year, and often 24 hours a day in all weathers.

The varied tasks included keeping vermin down with trap-setting, night-watching, and tending to rearing pens with the constant threat of injury, or even death, at the hands of vicious poachers. In the past a gamekeeper may occasionally have had some sympathy for those struggling to support large families, but today the threat tends to be different, with the traditional 'amateur' poacher having been replaced by highly organised mobile gangs who may stop at nothing.

Gamekeepers' skills were often handed down from father to son, and there is no finer example than that of James Hicks who was the last of the gamekeepers on the Trentham Estate. He was born at Moor Park, near Ludlow in Shropshire on 6th January 1864, and his father was gamekeeper to Sir William Broadwood whose family had amassed their wealth from the manufacture and sale of pianos.

Although not compulsory, young James was sent to school, but he didn't like the strict regime, having witnessed fellow pupils being thrashed with a birch rod for the slightest of misdemeanours. Consequently, the lad would often play truant and discreetly follow his father into the woods and fields, only revealing himself when it was too late to be returned to the classroom. His father, somewhat annoyed, yet amused, would often admonish him, but generally forgave him as he could appreciate where his son's interests lay. Thus the boy roamed around the countryside and knew nature from infancy - the changing seasons, and the growing life of trees, etc. Birds and animals were an open book to him, and he soon became acquainted with their names, haunts and habits. No roar of aircraft nor motor vehicle disturbed the lovely Shropshire countryside then, and his only means of transport was a horse, or a penny farthing cycle without rubber tyres.

Summer days were occupied gathering in the harvest. This was before the advent of farm machinery, and corn and hay was cut by teams of men using scythes. Thirst was quenched with home brewed cider or beer, the farmer delivering casks to the field. In later life, James recalled an occasion when he was given the task of cleaning out a number of cider barrels, the dregs being thrown to the pigs. Having guzzled the swill, they would stand around for a few minutes as if in a trance, then advance a step or two, stagger, then collapse into a drunken slumber!

At the age of 12 he commenced regular work as an odd job man, working for a local farmer-publican, but shortly afterwards gained employment as a 'bricklayer's boy' (or apprentice) in Ludlow. Walking the two and a half miles into town daily to commence work at 6.30am, he stayed in this occupation until the age of 21.

In December 1885, after working outside in wet conditions, his father developed pneumonia and died suddenly, resulting in James becoming the principal breadwinner. It was a hard struggle to make ends meet. The family consisted of his mother and 10 children, the youngest being 8 months old. Fortunately, the new owner of Moor Park, Major Forster, appreciating that James had assisted his father on occasion, offered him the vacant position. So James readily agreed to the proposal and left bricklaying for gamekeeping. The move meant that the family were allowed to remain in the house which formed part of the estate.

In his early 20s, James main recreation was the local army volunteers. He is said to have 'cut a fine figure' in his brilliant red uniform, and he enjoyed marching on parade behind his unit's band. Summer camps he found a delight, living under canvas, having free meals and participating in shooting competitions and organised sports. On occasion, he is also known to have exhibited his strength by lifting a 56lb weight in each hand.

After a few years he decided to seek a post where he could gain more experience of his work and secured employment on Lord Cholmondley's estate near Whitchurch. It is here that he was to meet his future wife Sarah Ann Clutton. Still seeking more experience and greater responsibility, he then moved to Lord Combermere's estate at Combermere Abbey for a brief period before transferring to Hardwick, the estate of Sir Joseph Bibby. In 1899 he married Sarah who by this time was working as a ladies' maid in London.

James Hicks joined the Duke of Sutherland's staff in 1901, having been head-hunted whilst employed by Lord Stafford at Beech. However, he did not move to Trentham until 1927. Although by this period he was in his 60s, he remained fit and strong and it is recorded that even then he was capable of lifting a 2 cwt sack of corn from a cart and carrying it into a store! Residing rent free in a detached property in the pleasant surroundings of Trentham Park, his main responsibilities were maintaining order in the park including locking and unlocking the huge iron gates, keeping fences repaired, and tending to the famous historic deer herd. For this he was paid £2 weekly. His own time was occupied looking after his garden and poultry, and the continuation of open air life undoubtedly resulted in prolonging James' good health. Occasionally deer had to be culled, with their skins being cured and made into rugs. Antlers were mounted and hung. In 1930, James and Ann took their first holiday, a weekend break at Llandudno - and the first time that they had seen the sea!

Among his other interests, James Hicks made homemade wines. According to his grand-daughter Vera, these included rhubarb, dandelion, and also wheat which was 'the colour of whisky and very potent!' Tony Gregory recalls that one day whilst taking his dog for a walk through King's Wood he saw the gamekeeper drilling holes in a silver birch tree and then putting a jar underneath. Having seen this done on a number of previous occasions, curiosity got the better of him and he enquired what the man was doing. The gamekeeper explained that he was tapping the tree to make wine. This procedure, he maintained, could only be done in the Spring when the sap was rising, and after drilling, the holes were plugged so that the tree didn't die. It was understood that the wine was 'a favourite of Prince Albert's' and having tried a sample, Tony could understand why!

Tony was also a keen fisherman at Trentham and the gamekeeper supplied him with red squirrel tails on occasion, used for fly fishing. He remembers seeing estate workers shooting magpies and crows as they attempted to take the young ducklings from the lakeside. Trentham was also renowned for its large pike, and at one time Tony had witnessed one take an unsuspecting duckling.

In 1936, the Hicks family were obliged to move as a golf course was being constructed in Trentham Park, and the property in which they were living was required for the club house. Their new residence was in the estate's mews type development then known as The Courtyard situated on Park Drive. This was not so isolated from neighbours, and for the first time they had the benefit of gas lighting, making paraffin lamps redundant! (The property has in recent years been converted into private luxury apartments).

World War II saw the evacuation of the London Clearing Banks to Trentham Gardens, and the requisition under emergency powers of areas of Trentham Park. In June 1940 the parkland suddenly became transformed into a transit camp for thousands of foreign troops including a large number of that unique fighting force, the French Foreign Legion. A large quantity of bell tents were erected but the sheer scale of operation in organising the vast camp meant that, at least for a time, many were forced to sleep under the trees. Whilst some had lost everything, others were fully armed with their adrenalin still flowing, having been more or less thrust into the area from the battlefield. The park was no longer James' domain, with security fencing having been hurriedly erected and the police and military taking control of the area.

The park gates and railings surrounding the front of The Courtyard were requisitioned for recycling as part of the war effort. It is understood that James was quite upset at the removal of the railings in front of his home, and he replaced them with rambling roses planted alongside the boundary walls. The property became renowned for its annual shows of blooms and, in turn, was renamed 'The Rosary'. With less responsibility now, James concentrated his energy on his beloved garden which was situated on the opposite side of the road and bordering the River Trent. (This area of land has recently been redeveloped with private housing).

Early in the war period James had to be admitted to the local hospital for an operation. During his hospitalisation the complex was bombed and he later recalled being awakened by '*a terrific roaring explosion. The place was in darkness with nurses and patients calling to each other before lighting was eventually restored*'. Apparently, an enemy aircraft had dropped a bomb on an operating theatre which had only been commissioned a week earlier. It is believed that the target was the Michelin factory or Shelton Bar.

The operation was successful, but he had developed cancer. Nonetheless, throughout hostilities with the aid of medication, he carried on maintaining his garden, wheeling barrow loads of apples and manure etc, but having seen Britain achieve victory, he passed away on 13th July 1946, his death bringing another phase in the history of Trentham to a close.

James Hicks, both photos taken in 1927 on the Duke of Sutherland's estate at Sutton Green. *Courtesy Vera Hicks*

Sarah Hicks, wife of James, in 1929 with pet albino deer outside the Gamekeeper's Cottage. *Courtesy Vera Hicks*

A photograph in 1938 of the courtyard at Park Drive, Trentham. The Hicks family moved here from the cottage in the Park.
Courtesy Vera Hicks

The Gamekeeper's Cottage, home of the Hicks family in Trentham Park, 1929. The property is now the club house of Trentham Park Golf Club.
Courtesy Vera Hicks

Winter and deer in Trentham Park in 1935.
Courtesy Vera Hicks

Brough Lane off Longton Road c.1911.
The property in the left foreground presently houses the local post office. *Courtesy Mrs Barbara Hobson*

An early 20th century view of Stone Road looking south towards Trentham Gardens.
Sadly these half-timbered buildings are no longer in existence. *Courtesy Mrs Barbara Hobson*

8. THATCHED HERITAGE

England is blessed with a rich architectural heritage. From the large and the glorious to the small and the curious, the architects and builders of past generations have bequeathed us a most wonderful legacy. Among some of the most popular and eye catching properties are those which are thatched, and it is perhaps easy to understand why they have remained a favourite. It has also, of course, resulted in the survival of the ancient craft of thatching. In fact, it is surprising to learn that, even today, this remains big business, the reeds being exported from such areas as Norfolk.

Trentham is most fortunate in still possessing a pair of these 'chocolate box ' properties, and these are believed to be the only thatched properties surviving in the City of Stoke-on-Trent. Numbered as 18 and 22 overlooking Longton Road, the cottages are within a short distance of the Ash Green roundabout and are Grade II listed buildings. Having said that, surprisingly, a large highway directional sign is erected on the footway to the front of the properties which, in my view, detracts from their character and appearance. In an otherwise picturesque setting with land rising to The Ley at the rear, the two properties are thought to have originally been built as three dwellings until conversion, and are believed to date from the 17th Century.

On average, a thatched ridge needs replacing every 10 or 12 years, but the remainder of a roof can survive for 45 - 60 years. According to Fred Powell who lives at Ivy House (18 Longton Road) *'the sunshine does more damage to the thatch because it dries up the reed which eventually cracks. The rain keeps it supple and stops it cracking.'* The roofs of the cottages were rethatched with reed in the summer of 2003. The contractor was master thatcher Wayne Halfpenny of Altrincham and his two sons. Trevor Norcop of the adjoining property (Ivy Cottage, 22 Longton Road) recalls the replacement reeds being delivered in two loads of 5,000 bundles (or yelms) and the cottages were surrounded in scaffolding for the period of the work.

Trevor also explained that when the roof areas were stripped for rethatching, early methods of construction were revealed - for example, hand-made nails and wooden dowels were discovered - and that the rafters comprised complete segments of trees which had been chopped, and not sawn. Also, beneath the floorboards, square joists were found on top of round posts. Such evidence tends to confirm the belief that parts of the properties do date from the 17th Century and, from his own research, Trevor Norcop believes that they were built c.1650. However, the fretwork porches (or orne) to the front of each dwelling date from the 18th Century. These were often added during the period to create an 'ornamental' or 'picturesque' effect.

At some point, both Ivy House and Ivy Cottage came into the ownership of the Duke of Sutherland, as they were included in the extensive list of properties sold by auction following the family's formal abandonment of Trentham as a permanent residence. The sales details described the estate as *'one of the finest residential, agricultural and sporting domains in the UK'* and the auction of 560 lots was conducted over a number of days in October 1919 by Barber & Sons at the Kings Hall, Stoke-on-Trent.

Many of the properties were let to employees, or former employees of the estate. It is understood that previously the Estate Factor resided at Ivy House, with a carpenter being his neighbour at Ivy Cottage. The comprehensive brochure confirmed that *'in nearly every case, the tenancy is an annual one running from Lady Day (25th March) to Lady Day.'* The lengthy document also explained that *'many of the rents given in the sales particulars are extremely low, and should not be taken as representing the letting value of the premises.'*[1]

At the time of the auction, Ivy House was detailed as Lot 228, and described as *'very picturesque'*, possessing 4 bedrooms, 2 sitting rooms, entrance hall, kitchen and pantry, with front and back staircases. Outbuildings included a wash house, dairy, coal house, wc, stables, cow house, 2 pig stys, and land comprising a flower garden, kitchen garden and a detached allotment. Ivy Cottage (Lot 227) was decribed as a *'prettily situated'* property containing 3 bedrooms, an entrance lobby, sitting room, living room, scullery and pantry with outbuildings of coal house,wc, pig sty and tool shed.

Subsequently, both Ivy House and Ivy Cottage came into the ownership of local businessman Harry Hemmings, who resided in the former. Described as a 'shrewd entrepreneur' with varied interests, his business 'empire' included highway engineering, and in 1929 one of his employees became his tenant next door at Ivy Cottage. This was Trevor's grandfather, William Samuel Norcop who drove the giant steam rollers for his landlord and employer, and in moving next door to his boss began the family association with Ivy Cottage which continues today.

In later years, the property became known as the residence of motor cycle specialist Samuel Robert Norcop (Trevor's father). A talented man, he was originally a baker, before moving to nearby Wedgwood Memorial College as a chauffeur/gardener. According to his daughter Janet, the motor cycle 'business' originated as a hobby, but as his expertise with the machines became common knowledge in the area, and his reputation grew, so did the number of customers! Many recall observing Mr Norcop engaged in tuning or repairing a machine as they walked by the Longton Road property.

Next door, Ivy House was renowned for its garden. With having such an extensive area to cultivate, Harry Hemmings was able to fully diversify with flowers, fruit and vegetables. In addition to the lawns and flower garden at the front of the property, he also possessed a kitchen garden to the side and rear, and a detached allotment situated on the opposite side of Longton Road. A wartime edition of the Sentinel featured a photograph of Mr Hemmings standing in his plot of 4,000 onions [2] - perhaps part of the 'Dig for Victory' campaign, when the public were encouraged to grow their own vegetables as part of the war effort. Part of Trentham Gardens was also brought under cultivation at this period, to produce a patriotic output of potatoes, cabbages etc.

Trentham had other thatched properties which unfortunately were lost for various reasons in the 1960s. These included a picturesque block of 4 dwellings of varying sizes on the south side of Longton Road near to Ivy House and Ivy Cottage. Also part of the former Trentham Estate, they were described in the 1919 auction details as having large gardens and a grass forecourt. It is believed that the properties were demolished when the widening of Longton Road took place in the late 1960s. The site of the houses was subsequently redeveloped with a petrol filling station (at the time of writing, the latter is being replaced with premises for the Fast Lane Company). The New Inn was another thatched property which was lost during the period. Formerly situated in New Inn Lane, many believe that the highway took its name from the property, a reasonable assumption.

Thankfully, as listed buildings, Ivy House and Ivy Cottage survive as important parts of our area's heritage, although even they lost some land, when, in the name of 'progress', Longton Road was widened.

NOTES

1. Sales details of the former Trentham Estate (Volume I), October 1919
2. *The Sentinel* 21st August 1943

These thatched cottages stood in Longton Road and were demolished in the 1960s.
The cottage on the right was a general store. The site is presently occupied by the Fast Lane Garage.
Courtesy Mary Bratby

The rear of Ivy Cottage, No 22 Longton Road, Trentham during WW II, with Anderson shelter in the foreground.
Courtesy Trevor Norcop

Harry Hemmings at the front of Ivy Cottage, No 18 Longton Road, Trentham in August 1943.
Courtesy Trevor Norcop

Harry Hemmings at the rear of Ivy Cottage, in his vegetable garden.
Courtesy Trevor Norcop

Master thatcher, Wayne Halfpenny, working on Nos 18 and 22 Longton Road in June 2003.
Courtesy The Sentinel

Thatching in progress at 18 and 22 Longton Road (Grade II listed buildings) June 2003.
Photograph by author

Below:
The thatched New Inn from which New Inn Lane derived its name, in 1968 just prior to demolition. The former NSR railway bridge can also be seen to the left.
Courtesy Mrs G. Cook

Longton Road looking towards Ash Green.
Courtesy Mrs Barbara Hobson

Trentham Golf Clubhouse, Barlaston Old Road.
Courtesy Mrs Barbara Hobson

Ash Green looking towards Trentham Gardens. *Courtesy Mrs Barbara Hobson*

Trentham Parish Council 1922. *Courtesy Mrs T. Shanahan*
Seated back: H. Selwood, J. Sant, A.V. Reynolds, P. Chadwick.
Front: T. Holdcroft, A.H.C. Wenger, W.H. Stevens, J.E. Hood, E. Lancaster.
Inset: Left, E.J. Pidduck JP. Right, J. Brooks.

The bridge to nowhere - the NSR's steel bridge over Stone Road which was intended to extend the line to Pool Dam. It was demolished in WWII. Trentham Park station was to the left of this photo. *Courtesy Mrs G. Cook*

The railway bridge over the A34 Stone Road, Trentham, in 1914. With the then small amount of traffic, children often used the area beneath it as a play area. *Courtesy Mrs T. Shanahan*

9. THE BRIDGE TO NOWHERE

For its size in the early 20th Century, Trentham was perhaps unique in having two railway stations (three, if Hanford Road Halt is included!).

The original main line station off Longton Road was provided by the North Staffordshire Railway (NSR) in 1849, but the buildings were later replaced in 1851 at the instigation of the Duke of Sutherland to the design of Sir Charles Barry to complement Trentham Hall. As a result, it has been said that no other small railway station could match the architectural grandeur of Trentham. Its accommodation included the Duke's private waiting room, complete with a marble fireplace. The buildings were demolished following closure of the station in the mid 1960s.

In 1910, the railway company opened its Trentham Park branch. With a halt known as Hanford Road, the line was carried over a bridge at New Inn Lane and across to Trentham Park station. The drive to the former station may be seen off A34 Stone Road opposite to its junction with Whitmore Road. The line was built in an attempt to exploit the use of NSR's rail motor cars (3rd class, hand baggage only). An innovation of the Edwardian years, the rail motor cars were popular with daytrippers, and said to look 'splendid' in the NSR maroon livery. These were used on certain routes to capitalise on the potential tripper market (eg market days), and Trentham with its vast deer park was regarded by the railway company as a popular excursion destination.

The branch may have enjoyed better fortunes but for the onset of the Great War, Hanford Road Halt already having been closed in 1913. The war also delayed plans to extend the line via Pool Dam, Newcastle-under-Lyme to Silverdale following the course of the valley around the growing suburbs of Hanford and Trent Vale. In the meantime, as part of the proposals, a 70ft steel bridge had been erected 16ft above the carriageway of what is now the A34 Stone Road, but the scheme was abandoned in 1923. The bridge remained as a mute reminder of past inspirations but was eventually dismantled for scrap during World War II.

However, the Trentham Park branch itself became busier than ever during the Second World War. In addition to a daily goods service, the line was servicing the Central Clearing House (CCH) evacuated to the Trentham Gardens Ballroom for the duration. Over 900 members of the CCH staff arrived at Trentham on 26th August 1939 in two special trains from the capital. At the time, this move formed an integral part of a pre-planned evacuation of Government Departments and businesses from London as a result of defence experts' assumptions that war would commence with an immediate aerial bombardment by the Germans of the capital and other major cities.

Basically, the reasons for Trentham Gardens being chosen for the relocation of the Clearing Banks are two fold. Firstly, it was considered to be 'a safe area' by the Treasury. Secondly, it had to be capable of being fully serviced by the postal and rail authorities which, in turn, had to be able to guarantee that the 7,000 or so letters received daily could be transported and delivered with 'reasonable expedition.' Thus, the close proximity of Trentham Park station was an important factor in the choice of evacuation location. The number of cheques cleared at Trentham rose from slightly less than 322 million in 1940, to in excess of 346 million in 1946. Consequently, the CCH's contribution to the war effort should not be under-estimated.[1]

During the period of hostilities the branch line was also used to convey special 'casualty' trains. On arrival at Trentham Park station wounded servicemen would be transferred to convoys of ambulances which would then proceed with motor cycle escort to designated hospitals. After appropriate medical treatment, a number would have been discharged to No. 122 Military Convalescent Depot in Trentham Park, one of the largest such establishments in the country during World War II. The convalescents, together with numbers of hospital based wounded servicemen, were familiar sights in the area. At local events such as football matches, it was not unusual for them to receive a standing ovation.

The return of peace saw the station renamed Trentham Gardens on 7th October 1946. Although nationalisation of the railways in 1948 had little effect on locomotive working or train operation, gradually economies resulted in line or branch closures. Trentham Park fell into this category, closing on 1st October 1957[2], with the main line station closing in the early 1960s.

On closure of the branch line and removal of the track, the land became a popular informal walkway. This was also utilised by staff and pupils of the nearby Trentham Church of England School for nature walks. Finally, in 1974, the branch line land was sold off in plots and incorporated into gardens, the exception being that at the end of Churchill Avenue which was redeveloped for a Scout and Guide Headquarters.

NOTES

1. Graham Bebbington, *Trentham at War* (Churnet Valley Books), Chapters 2 & 12.
2. Rex Christiansen & R. W. Miller, *The North Staffordshire Railway* (David & Charles) p 304

The bridge in the process of construction.

The railway bridge, New Inn Lane, Trentham, taken in 1968. Brassington's Farm is to the right.
Courtesy Mrs G. Cook

The former Trentham Station off Longton Road. It was designed, at the instigation of the Duke of Sutherland, by Sir Charles Barry.

Courtesy Mrs B. Hobson

The railway bridge over New Inn Lane in the process of demolition in the mid-1970s. Hanford Road Halt, which closed in 1913, was to the right.

Courtesy Mrs G. Cook

The former Lord Abercrombie pub, now demolished and the site redeveloped with housing.
Photograph by the author in 1978 on the day it finally closed.

George Harper, extreme right, and some of his Kodak colleagues from the Central Clearing House, Trentham.
Seen here with local residents at the rear of the Staffordshire Knot in High Street, Hanford (now Mayne Street).

10. PARKER'S 'PURGE' & LOCAL HOSTELRIES

Parker's, Joules and Bents were household names in North Staffordshire during the last century. They were the 'big boys' of the local licensed trade, owning hundreds of pubs in and around the area. Today, whenever there is a discussion about the beers of yesteryear, their names are guaranteed to be mentioned.

It was not unusual in the 1950s for some companies to still be delivering goods by means of horse transport. Parker's Brewery was no exception, and their horse-drawn wagons were a popular sight in the Potteries area. The wagons displayed the company colours of cherry red, with the name Parker's in gold leaf on a circular crest and wheatsheaf on top. There are many who can remember hearing the familiar 'clop-clop' of the huge hooves of the beautiful great dray horses on the highway as they went about replenishing the pubs. Some recall that on hearing the sound, they would hurry out of the house with a bucket to collect any manure which may have been deposited in the street, for use on the garden or allotment!

Parker's, which at one time had an empire of 468 pubs, produced draught mild and bitter, Parker's Burslem bitter in bottles and a milk stout. The draught bitter was affectionately known as Parker's 'Purge' as it was strongly reputed to work on the potters and miners by *'cleansing their systems of all the muck and dirt!'*

The old Staffordshire Knot at Hanford was a popular Parker's pub. Situated at what is now a dwelling at 165 Stone Road, its regular patrons during World War II included staff from the London Banks' Central Clearing House (CCH), Trentham Gardens and personnel from HMS Daedalus II, the Royal Navy Artificer Training Establishment (RNATE) at Clayton Hall. The CCH staff at this time were living around Stoke-on-Trent, particularly in the Hanford, Trentham and Trent Vale areas. Southerner George Harper was one of the Kodak staff employed at the CCH, and he was renting a house - 'Highbury' in Wilson Road, Hanford - from Stoke City striker Tommy Sale. Older supporters remember this popular player as a goalscorer *'with a lethal left foot!'*

Courtesy The Sentinel

Tommy Sale, prolific Stoke City goalscorer with a lethal left foot.

By coincidence, George Harper's son, Ron, was at HMS Daedalus II at Clayton Hall for a period. He had completed a seven and a half year apprenticeship before joining the service, and attended an 18 week armament fitters' course at Clayton. He later returned to the establishment as an instructor. Although the Fleet Air Arm personnel frequented the pubs of Newcastle, depending on where they were billeted, some patronised the smaller hostelries in the suburbs, such as the Staffordshire Knot. Although forbidden by the Navy to drink or smoke under the age of 18 years, FAA apprentices did, nevertheless, frequent pubs. However, in doing so, they had to be alert because Navy Police patrols often appeared

Courtesy Mrs Barbara Hobson

Trentham Hotel.

unannounced. When such a situation occurred, it was not unusual for certain sympathetic landlords to temporarily hide the boys in the cellar!

In 1945 Mr and Mrs William Cooper moved into No.1 High Street (now Mayne Street), Hanford, renting the property from Parker's Brewery. When that company was purchased by Ind Coope & Allsopp in 1948, they decided to replace the Staffordshire Knot with new premises, to be built on the corner of Church Lane and High Street. This site included the property formerly leased to the Cooper family. As a consequence, the Coopers were transferred into the old Stone Road pub in 1956 which, over a period of time, they converted to residential accommodation.

The terraced property required total refurbishment - redecoration, complicated rewiring and amendments to the layout, before it was successfully transformed into the present 5 bedroomed house. Fortunately, Bill Cooper was a builder! However, he recalls that during refurbishment, he removed 11 wallpapers from some walls, and all electrics had to be rewired from the existing board behind the bar. Bill states that, in addition to the bar areas, the former pub had a cellar from where the beer was piped, a music and games room at the rear, and toilets in the yard. There was also a serving hatch for outdoor sales to the High Street rear access.

Another licensed premises popular with Trentham folk was the nearby Lord Abercrombie Inn in Mayne Street. In its early days it was named the Ralph Abercrombie Inn, but local residents also referred to it as 'The Soldier.' Named after a military hero who died defeating the French at Aboukir Bay in 1801, the beerhouse opened c.1830. According to local historian Andrew Dobraszczyc, the premises were occupied from 1838-1871 by Israel Wood, described as a shoemaker and publican. In 1881, the pub was still being managed by his widow Sarah at the age of 74!

In the 20th Century, the tiny public house was to claim fame as the last drinking place of the murderer Michael Bassett. Bassett was responsible for the deaths of 3 young French tourists in the

Courtesy Mary Bratby

Longton Road looking towards Hem Heath, Trentham Hotel on right, 1913, by photographer T.G. Adie of Stone.

Delamere Forest in the summer of 1970. According to John Abberley of the Sentinel, it was the biggest crime story at the time. Having shot them, he drove back to the Potteries where he called at the Lord Abercrombie, one of his favourite pubs, even playing the piano there. He later travelled to Barlaston Downs where he died by his own hand, having confessed to the murders in farewell notes.

The public house, which stood approximately opposite to the entrance to Briarbank Close, was eventually closed in 1978, having been acquired by the City Council from Allied Breweries under the terms of a Compulsory Purchase Order. The premises were subsequently demolished, and the site and adjoining area redeveloped with housing.

The Bulls Head public house at the junction of Mayne Street and Bankhouse Road dates from 1938. It was built on the site of a pub of the same name, but locals also referred to it as 'Ye Old Coaching House No. 3'. When it reopened its doors to the public, the Newcastle Times (2nd September 1938) defined the hostelry as being *'the most remarkable hotel for miles around.'* Rebuilt in the Tudor style, the newspaper described the premises as being *'half timbered with characteristic ornamented gables and steep sloping roofs and tastefully tiled.'* The front page report went on to further detail the hotel as being *'sumptuously carpeted'* with *'nothing imitative about the materials - carving is genuine carving and oak is solid oak.'* The design was by Ind Coope & Allsopp's own architect, W. Blair and the newspaper reported that the company considered the hotel to be *'one of their most magnificent buildings.'* It is sad, therefore, that the building has been so unsympathetically extended in the latter part of the last century.

At the time of the reopening, the licensee was reported as *'the popular and respected'* Mr B. Vere Abbott. Having served in the Great War as a Regimental Sergeant Major, he was also the veteran of campaigns in South Africa and the Boxer Rebellion in China.

The Bulls Head was a popular drinking haunt of the bandsmen who appeared at the Trentham

Gardens Ballroom. In the 'glory days' of dancing and the big band era, two bands could often be found appearing on the same programme. A 'top band' such as that of Joe Loss or Ted Heath would have been supported by resident local band the Norman Jones Orchestra or Reg Bassett's.

When a band was on its break, the sidesmen would often leave the ballroom to quench their thirst at the Bulls Head. As it happened, on the evening of 11th October 1963, the Beatles appeared at Trentham supported by the Ken Jones Orchestra. The orchestra played their normal routine until 9.00 pm when the Beatles were due on stage, but the 'Fab Four' arrived late, not arriving until 9.20pm. According to former Ken Jones saxophonist Percy le Rolland, although the orchestra carried on playing until the group was ready, this was not popular as *valuable drinking time was being lost at the Bulls Head!'*

The village of Trentham, of course, had its own public houses, their history being a little complicated. The earliest reference in the Parish Records to occupations linked to the licensed trade appears to be that of the death in August 1733 of Henry Mountford, Innkeeper. Unfortunately, no details are given of the hostelry concerned.

In the 19th Century, the Trentham Inn was the foremost in the village. Standing on the main road (now the A34) opposite Whitmore Road (or Dog Kennel Lane), it was more than a village pub. The premises were multifunctional, serving not only as a drinking establishment, but variously as a Magistrates' Court and a public meeting place. Various societies conducted their business there, including the North Staffordshire Reform Association. The North Staffordshire Mercury in its edition of 12th December 1840 carries the statutory notice for the organisation's AGM to be held at the premises. The same newspaper in its edition of 2nd February 1833 gives notice to *the tenants and friends'* of His Grace the Duke of Sutherland, that a dinner will be held at the Trentham Inn *'in honour of his Grace being promoted to the Dukedom' - 'tickets to be had at the bar of the Inn, for which an early application is respectfully recommended.'*

In 1867 the Trentham Inn was closed and its license transferred to the site now occupied by the Trentham Hotel in Longton Road. A public house known as the Roebuck Inn had previously occupied the land, but this had been destroyed by fire two years earlier. The Staffordshire Times & Newcastle Pioneer in its edition of 2nd September 1865 carries a brief report of the incident and of the innkeeper, Mr Brassington and his family, having been rescued by two passers-by.

The new premises in Longton Road became known as the Trentham New Inn (sometimes the Sutherland Arms) and the move was seen by some as a deliberate ploy on the part of the Duke to remove the sale of alcohol further out of the village, and away from the area of the Hall.

As for the former pub premises on the main road, they became the stables of the North Staffs Hunt where it is understood that up to 60 hunters were stabled at times. The pack of 50-60 hounds was kennelled nearby in premises off Whitmore Road in the area now occupied by Fairway. Surviving records give the impression that no expense was spared to maintain the horses and dogs at Trentham. The period is still recalled by the many residents who continue to refer to Whitmore Road as 'Dog Kennel Lane.'

The stables of the North Stafford Hunt (the former Trentham Inn) in Stone Road, Trentham 1919.

Bebbington collection

A bowls match in progress at the Trentham Hotel, 1919.

Bebbington collection

The Priory, Trentham. Home of the Wenger family c. 1948.   *Courtesy Mrs Isabelle Newton*

The Priory, Trentham, from the drive.   *Courtesy Mrs Isabelle Newton*

11. WENGERS & THE PRIORY

Until the middle of the last century, a large attractive property was situated to the rear of the Sutherland mausoleum on the A34 Stone Road, Trentham. Believed to have dated from the late 18th Century, the Priory - a former parsonage, was probably built in three phases. By the front door was a large early 20th Century conservatory, renowned for its displays of geraniums, one variety appropriately being 'Priory Pink.' Due to its secluded position, only those who had business there, saw the house. Access was via a lengthy rhododendron lined drive abutting the north side of the mausoleum, but neither the house nor its extensive gardens could be viewed from the main road.

The property was purchased in 1911 from the Duke of Sutherland by Mr Adolph Henry Charles Wenger (1877-1954), and he subsequently added a further 21 acres. The resulting Wenger estate consisted of an area roughly bordering Stone Road, Allerton Road, New Inn Lane, Brook Road, Brinsley Avenue and Longton Road, with the exception of the properties already built along the lengths of those roads.

Adolph Wenger was descended from an old and noble Swiss family. His father, Albert Francis Wenger (1837-1924), was born at Lausanne on Lake Geneva and was the founder of the famous company of Wengers Ltd of Etruria. Having learned the art of pottery at Nyon, he came to England in 1869 initially establishing himself in business at Cobridge, before having a large factory, with modern laboratories, built at Etruria in 1900. Naturalised in 1893, he was a practical potter, connoisseur and successful water-colour painter, and regarded as one of the most remarkable men in the industry. Considered to be a genius by some, he pioneered the manufacture of colours and chemicals for the pottery, tile, brick, glass, and vitreous enamel industries. In addition, he introduced numerous modern improvements in pottery manufacture including vapourisers for spraying colours onto ware, and was the first manufacturer of lustres in the country. He also introduced liquid gold and before World War I, Wengers were the only manufacturer of the product in England. His obituary described him as *'an extraordinary personality and a man who had done a lot for the pottery industry, and who amongst other things had foreseen the growth of studio pottery.'*

On the death of his father, Adolph Wenger assumed the role of Chairman and Managing Director of the company. Born in Hanley, he was educated at Newcastle High School and later, on the continent. Like his father, Adolph was to become one of North Staffordshire's leading industrialists and public figures. In the course of a busy life, he also found time for public work, being appointed a Justice of the Peace in 1929 and serving as High Sheriff of the County in 1935-36. For a period, he was also a member of Newcastle Town Council, and before nationalisation of the hospitals was a Life Governor of the North Staffordshire Royal Infirmary. A pioneer motorist, he was competing in events in 1903, his other interests including the North Staffordshire Hunt and golf.

Foreign travel, and a mind both inquiring and cultivating, gave Adolph Wenger an exceptionally wide range of interests, particularly art, and this was reflected in the contents of the Priory. It was finely furnished with both antique and modern furniture, a valuable collection of historic ware and paintings. Access to a cellar was from the ground floor. On the ground floor the accommodation included a large kitchen (with larder & pantry), a sewing room, large and small dining rooms, and a drawing room. There was also a substantial ballroom with a full sized billiard table in a separate section of the room, and a library comprising a fine collection of books reflecting local interest including first editions by Pape, Bennett and Warrillow.

A wide hallway ran the length of the house, boasting a tiled floor reputed to have been the personal gift of Herbert Minton (1793-1858). Carpeted in a red patterned style it contained, amongst other things, a magnificent huge three bears hat and coat stand, carved from one piece of lime from the Black Forest. The hall gave access to five rooms to the right, all of which looked out onto a terrace. Sleeping accommodation comprised seven bedrooms on the first floor, and the bathrooms and toilets were said to be *'interesting with elderly but expensive fittings'*.

Outside, on the south side, were formally laid out gardens terraced down to a tennis court and a summer house. At the top of the terrace was a huge cedar tree which survives today. On the north side a farm formed part of the estate. Credit must be given to Adolph's wife, Isabelle (Belle), who created *'a wonderful, homely atmosphere,'* for the family that included their four children - James, Violet, Reg and Marguerita (Rita). According to Mrs Isabelle Newton, the daughter of Violet and the Rev'd Ivo D. W. Knowles, *'the Priory was a lovely house'* and her grandparents *'loved having their grandchildren there, and there was no fuss if anything was broken.'* Her brother, Thomas, agreed recalling that they played outside in the wonderful garden, or tried their hand on the tennis court. In the winter, or if the weather was poor, they would have the run of the house until grandfather returned home. The grandchildren also liked to visit the kitchen where several cats enjoyed the range and tolerated Aunt Rita's dog.

Thomas also reveals that Friday afternoons were a highlight, being always marked by visits to the Priory when he was small, the weekly family gathering of daughters, daughters in law, and grandchildren. Together with his mother and sister, he regularly caught the 2.45 pm Newcastle-Trentham bus at Trent Vale or Flash Lane. His father who was the Vicar of Trent Vale, used to carry out his hospital visits on Friday afternoons and so arrived later at the Priory in a pre-war Morris 8 saloon which Thomas admits *'was somewhat down at heel compared to the other vehicles that would be parked there!'*

Afternoon tea was the order of the day, he recalls, with children being kept apart for some of the time. Grandfather Adolph did not return from the works until about 5.30pm and on arrival, he had a short rest during which time the children were under strict instructions to keep quiet! At the end of the day if the Vicar had been detained for some reason, Thomas, Isabelle and their mother would return home by catching the bus from the tunnel shelters at Trentham Gardens. Thomas has vivid memories of such journeys when the conductor stood with his back to the driver and used a coin to tap on the cab window to stop or start the bus, and how he announced to passengers 'CASSLE!' to distinguish his vehicle from the more frequent Stoke buses.

Nine members of staff were regularly employed at the Priory to serve the Wenger family, their quarters being on the north side. These comprised the cook, a butler, two housemaids, a governess and a part-time seamstress. Outside personnel consisted of Alfred Hart, the chauffeur, and two gardeners, all of whom lived nearby in tied accommodation at Paddock Cottages, off Longton Road. The estate's farmer, Mr Perkins, lived at the farm adjoining the main house. At times when extra staff were required, these would be brought in from the village.

Isabelle Newton recalls the rhododendron lined drive to the house as looking *gorgeous in season'*. An orchard was situated to the left of the drive, together with a kitchen garden and a hot house on the north east side of the house. Dead jays were hung on the fencing to deter other birds. All the gardens were well maintained by the gardening staff, and on the eastern side the hedges were manicured to resemble pottery kilns. These were affectionately referred to by the family as *'the potters' ovens'*. Fields surrounded the cultivated area and Thomas Knowles remembers haymaking one year when black moths were flying around in vast quantities.

In season, Adolph Wenger (known in North Staffordshire to his peers as 'The Boss'!) would proceed to the rose garden each morning and cut a bloom, inserting it in his buttonhole, before making his way to the office. The Wengers had a number of cars, including a Rolls Royce and Daimler, but Mr Wenger generally drove himself to the works daily. The chauffeur would convey Mrs Wenger, who could not drive, to required destinations such as Chester on shopping expeditions.

The farm and kitchen garden provided produce for the main house, and there was also a herd of cows and pigs. Kitchen staff made butter from the farm. The Wenger's daughter, Rita, kept horses on the premises, and regularly rode in Trentham Park.

At Christmas there was a wonderful atmosphere at the house with preparations beginning weeks in advance. Decorations usually took the form of festive foliage such as local holly, ivy and mistletoe, with a huge Christmas tree in the ballroom. The whole family assembled for the occasion and there were presents for everyone, including the staff. 'Christmas boxes' were also given to local tradesmen who attended regularly.

Carol singers from the village would visit the house, and be rewarded with mince pies etc. Vera Hicks and Trevor Norcop were among those who sang at the Priory, visiting with the church choir. They recollect walking up the dark drive to the house, and then assembling in the hall to sing festive songs and carols.

Thomas Knowles has outstanding memories of Christmas parties in the ballroom. The children sat at a table at the far end of the room from the billiard table and had jelly - *'a real treat in times of rationing!'* A large fire blazed in the room adding to the atmosphere, with seats near the hearth being well used by the adults. He remembers looking out of the window after dark with a cousin *'trying to show him Father Christmas flying away until next year.'* *'The problem was I couldn't see him!'* He also recalls Christmas lunch with the immediate family - *'Christmas pudding with silver sixpences.'*

During World War II, the ballroom fulfilled another important role. It was the nerve centre for Isabelle Wenger's sewing and knitting classes. Being well-liked in the village and a born organiser, the local ladies readily responded to her call to aid the war effort, and regular classes were held to provide comforts for the troops. Mrs Rosemary Bough (nee Bell) can recall her late mother participating in Mrs Wenger's group of volunteers, all dressed in white! Scarves and hats were made for the soldiers, and sales of work were also held there.

It is inevitable that nothing stays the same, and the wonderful atmosphere at the Priory came to an end in 1953 when Belle Wenger suffered a stroke. She was largely confined to her bedroom which faced Trentham Park. To make matters worse, her husband Adolph died the following year after a relatively short illness. Thomas Knowles says *'this changed life at the Priory considerably.'* A lift was installed to move his grandmother, and every effort was made to make her believe that life was continuing as normal. In reality, land assets owned by the family were sold off to meet debts, the services of a full-time nurse were engaged, and Mrs Wenger spent more and more time in her room. One great pleasure she had was watching the birds, blue tits in particular, on a small balcony to her bedroom. She passed away in January 1959.

Although there was talk of the house becoming a hotel, it was built over mining operations and subsidence was a factor. On 3rd and 4th June local estate agents Louis Taylor & Sons conducted a sale of the house contents from a large marquee on site. Shortly afterwards, the building was demolished, and the estate sold off for housing.

The demolition of the Priory saw the beginning of Trentham's housing boom. The former Wenger owned land was redeveloped to form the Priory Estate including Werburgh Drive. According to local authority records, this involved a number of developers including Theo Oakley Ltd, A. Hughes, W. H. Whitehurst, Morgan Builders Co, N. W. Midlands Builders, and Percy Bilton.

The new development, bringing in more families, required additional places above the capacity of the little nearby Victorian Church of England school. This resulted in its closure in 1962, the staff and pupils being transferred to the newly built Priory School in Jubilee Road. The building of the Priory Estate, and the demolition of the old school and its adjoining pseudo-Elizabethan buildings, meant the beginning of the end of Trentham as a typical English village.

However, readers with a keen eye and an interest in such matters may appreciate learning that evidence of the original Wenger Estate remains. The massive cedar tree continues to thrive, dominating the centre of Wenger Crescent, whilst a silver birch survives in a garden at the junction of Werburgh Drive and Wenger Crescent. Also, a large grit sandstone gate pillar on the walkway between A34 Stone Road and Coniston Place marks the site of the former entrance to the drive to the Priory.

Adolph and Isabelle Wenger taken in the garden of
their home, The Priory, with other views of the house
and garden. *Courtesy Mrs Isabelle Newton*

Inside The Priory. *Courtesy Mrs Isabelle Newton*

The Wenger children - James, Reg and Violet with Rita in the cart. 1911. *Courtesy Mrs Isabelle Newton*

Harvesting on the Wenger's estate in the 1940s. *Courtesy Mrs Isabelle Newton*

Below: Housing under construction in Werburgh Drive. Hem Heath Pit Head just visible in the distance. 1960. *Courtesy A. Cholerton.*

L.M.R. Sectional Council No. 2
BY-ELECTION 1956
Area No. 2

—●—

VOTE FOR

Driver

F. A. Cholerton

(Stoke-on-Trent)

The Official Candidate of the A.S.L.E. & F.

THE ONLY SOCIETY

which gives ONE HUNDRED PER CENT SERVICE
TO **YOUR** INTERESTS

Arthur Cholerton seen below with his image in process. Arthur was a record serving Chairman of the Staffordshire County Council. The bust is now in the Child Development Centre, Hilton Road, Hartshill, in the aptly named Cholerton Room.

Courtesy Mrs M. Shaffery

45074

Arthur Cholerton, CBE, on the
footplate of one of his beloved
locomotives.
Courtesy Mrs M. Shaffery

12. FROM FOOTPLATE TO COUNTY HALL

Former Trentham resident, the late Arthur Cholerton, was at the forefront of local politics for almost four decades, working tirelessly not only for the community he represented, but also for the wider benefit of Stoke-on-Trent and the County of Staffordshire.

I first had the privilege of meeting him in December 1986 at the launch of my book *Pit Boy to Prime Minister*. As this was the first published biography of local born Sir Joseph Cook (1860-1947), and was also being used to launch the 'Staffordshire Heritage' series, my publishers were keen to mark the occasion with a special ceremony at the Civic Offices, Newcastle-under-Lyme. This was accomplished with the generosity of the then Chief Executive, Alan G. Owen, and the Borough Council. Arthur was invited in his capacity as Chairman of Staffordshire County Council, but we were forewarned that it was unlikely that he would be available due to the number of engagements to which he was already committed. However, he did attend and it marked the beginning of a friendship which lasted until his death. After the book launch he continued to show a keen interest in my writing, and I sincerely hope that, perhaps in a small way, I was able to repay his kindness.

The son of a placer in the pottery industry, Frederick Arthur Cholerton was born at Penkhull on 15th April 1917. He was educated at the village school before commencing employment at Minton-Hollins for a brief period. However, perhaps with the intention of fulfilling a boyhood ambition, he joined the North Staffordshire Railway Company (or the 'Knotty') in 1934 as a trainee fireman. He remained working on the railways until his retirement by which time he was a qualified locomotive driver.

Once in a while Arthur would regale me with tales from the footplate in the glorious days of steam, particularly the period relating to World War II in which he appreciated that I had a keen interest. On one occasion he had the privilege of crewing the train carrying Prime Minister Winston Churchill, and this was driven onto the Trentham Park branch line where the Premier stayed overnight. In an effort to minimise noise, rubber shovels were used for stoking, and coal had earlier been broken into small pieces so that no hammering was required; and to keep down noise on the metal footplate, galoshes were issued to wear over the customary boots. Arthur also recalled that steam had to be maintained all night to keep the carriages warm, but at the same time the crew had to be careful not to get too much pressure on or the steam valve would have blown, which, in the circumstances, could have resulted in dismissal! Elaborate security measures were in place with a number of police and military personnel in attendance, and constant supplies of tea etc were required throughout the night. In the morning, the train crew caught sight of the Premier who acknowledged them. Tradition also has it that for some time afterwards, local residents searched the line for discarded cigar butts for souvenirs of the great man!

Arthur was also able to claim the privilege of crewing a royal train which he said was an experience in itself. Special rules applied, he explained, when working a royal train: *'Each section of the line had to be covered in a certain time with no excessive speed allowed.'* Stringent security measures were in operation throughout and it was not unusual to see police on bridges en route.

When air raids by enemy aircraft were spread all over the country during World War II, night trains travelled cautiously for fear of 'incidents' or 'mishaps' on the line, and it was on such an occasion that Arthur was on the crew of a London bound train when it was diverted into sidings at Nuneaton. From there, he witnessed the bombing of Coventry. On that night of 14th November 1940, German aircraft dropped 1,400 bombs on the city in a mission lasting more than 10 hours.

However, Arthur's favourite route was the Churnet Valley Line. Running through attractive countryside, it stretched from North Rode to Uttoxeter passing Rudyard Lake and Alton Towers. He contended that *'it was wonderful to work a train across that beautiful area, particularly when dawn was breaking and the birds were singing in the nearby woods.'* In complete contrast, Arthur's face also broke into a grin on telling me that in other parts of the nearby countryside during World War II it was not unusual to see American troops courting their girlfriends near to the line. It appeared that they had forgotten that they could be observed from the height of an engine cab!

Like many intelligent working class people, Arthur found an outlet for his talents in local politics. Having become involved with ASLEF, the railway union, he rose to national level and through his union work he forged his political career. In 1951, he joined Stoke-on-Trent City Council and continued up the ladder eventually becoming Leader of the Council. In 1971-72 he served as Lord Mayor and was especially delighted when Stoke City FC won the League Cup during his term of office.

Following local government reorganisation in 1974, he went on to represent the Great Fenton Ward on Staffordshire County Council. He served as Chairman of the authority for a record eight years (1981-89) and in 2000 the title of Hon. Alderman was conferred upon him in recognition of his eminent service as a County Councillor.

During his political career, he took a great deal of interest in planning matters and was a keen supporter of environmentally friendly schemes. In the 1980s, when landfill sites were in danger of becoming exhausted, he was concerned about the impact on the environment as rubbish levels increased. As a consequence, he visited various European cities with colleague Councillor Bill Austin in search of a waste incinerator for Stoke-on-Trent before settling on a £40m French installation. This remains one of his best remembered projects.

Also, during the period of his Chairmanship, links between Bremen and Staffordshire reached a major milestone, celebrating a 25th anniversary in 1987. The anniversary of the official opening of the German Military Cemetery at Cannock also coincided with the announcement of his intention to retire at the next election. As part of the commemoration arrangements it was decided to create the Bremen Room in County Buildings, Stafford and to record for posterity his outstanding service, the County Council commissioned a portrait of Arthur by the artist Oliver Campion FRSA. Fittingly, this now hangs in the Bremen Room.

Arthur's other achievements included spearheading an appeal to raise funds to build a child assessment unit at Hartshill for which he was instrumental in raising £750,000. In 1978 he was awarded a CBE for services to the community.

The 2003 edition of *Who's Who* lists Arthur Cholerton's recreations as sports, gardening, politics, and voluntary work for charities. However, he and his wife Ethel (nee Jackson) whom he married in 1939, also shared a love of words and the English language. He freely admitted to me that his wife could complete a crossword faster than he could, but the question of who was champion at the game of 'Scrabble' in the Cholerton household was likely to be strongly contested!

He died on 15th March 2004 at the age of 86 in Spratslade House Care Home, Dresden where he had been living for some months having been diagnosed as suffering from Alzheimer's Disease. His beloved wife Ethel predeceased him. The couple had one son who died in infancy.

Arthur Cholerton did tremendous work for the City of Stoke-on-Trent and the County of Staffordshire, and following his death many tributes were paid to him. John Crompton, past National President of the Society of Local Council Clerks, travelled with him on numerous occasions to London for meetings and conferences. He remembers Arthur as *'always very smart, a good delivery and a great knowledge of local government both at local and national level.'* John also recalls that if Arthur had two days or more of meetings in the capital, he always preferred to return home rather than sleep in a London hotel![1] His former colleague Bill Austin told me *'Arthur was 'a rare man' - he was an honest politician who kept his word!'*[2]

NOTES

1. John Crompton. Letter to author 27th March 2004.
2. Telephone interview with Bill Austin 2nd April 2004.

Young Brenda at the front with her mother
and cousin Jean, in 1931.

Brenda having a swingin' time at Trentham, 1939.

At Trentham Gardens around 1949.

Brenda, left, at Trentham in 2004
with Lynne Bebbington.

13. BRENDA STRUTS HER STUFF!

Brenda Meaney (now Mrs Kitching) was born in 1922 at the Station Inn, Tunstall where her father, Tom, was the publican. She made her debut on Christmas Day to the sound of carols being played outside by the local Salvation Army Band in a typically snowy yuletide scene. Freely admitting that her *'nostalgic recall is precious'* she has very fond memories of Trentham Gardens, and since childhood has regarded the venue as a *'magical and special place'.*

Her father's claim to fame was that he entered a cage containing two lions - and survived! A short distance from the pub was an area of wasteland where, on regular occasions, Pat Collins Fair would assemble for the enjoyment of the townsfolk. On their visits, the travellers patronised the pub and one day Pat Collins approached Tom Meaney with a startling proposition which, he claimed, would benefit them both. The plan was that Tom should enter the lion cage which, the astute showman maintained, would achieve extra receipts both at the pub and the fairground, from the resultant publicity. Although naturally reluctant, he was persuaded to accept the challenge following which, according to Brenda, *'you could not move'* because of the increased attendance. *'It was a tremendously successful stunt'* she said. After this she naturally regarded her father as a hero but in later years was disappointed to learn that the lions were, in fact, sedated! Brenda can recall a photograph of the event and of seeing her father appearing petrified, which is perhaps not surprising. The photograph was displayed for many years in the pub but sadly does not appear to have survived. Neither has any record of the extra business generated by the daring deed!

At the age of two, Brenda was diagnosed as having a TB hip. In an attempt to achieve a cure, she was initially admitted to Biddulph Grange from whence she was subsequently transferred to the 'Cripples' Home', Hartshill (later the Orthopaedic Hospital) where, for four years, she was *'anchored on iron frames and strapped to boards.'*

The Hartshill hospital owed its origins to the pioneering work of Millicent, Duchess of Sutherland. On coming to the area in 1884 as the young bride of the 4th Duke of Sutherland, she was shocked at seeing so many crippled children, particularly those that visited Trentham on the occasional outings known as 'cripples' treats'. Records show that on 30th July 1900 alone, 258 children were driven to Trentham in 'brakes.'[1] The Duchess was moved to found the Potteries & Newcastle Cripples' Guild which held its first annual general meeting at the Trentham Institute on 15th March 1901. The organisation subsequently founded, and ran, Stoke-on-Trent's main orthopaedic hospital at Hartshill following the purchase of the Longfields Estate in 1918. Longfields Hospital was officially opened by Sir Robert Jones and, on the same day, Sir Joseph Cook, the Silverdale-born former Australian Prime Minister, laid the foundation stone of the proposed operating theatre. Cook happened to be on a flying visit to the area during a break from the Imperial War Conference.

Whilst perhaps appearing inappropriate for the site of such an establishment Hartshill, with an elevation of over 500ft, was nevertheless considered *'a salubrious suburb'* at the time. Prevailing westerly winds generally blew the Potteries smoke from the area and Hartshill for some years had been favoured by a number of wealthy residents, including the great potter Herbert Minton who previously resided at Longfields.

When Longfields Hospital opened, Stoke-on-Trent was one of only a handful of towns to have made any provision for children needing orthopaedic treatment and, according to David Adams, the respected former Reference Librarian at Newcastle Library, in its early years the establishment was able to claim cures for 80% of both in-patients and out-patients.[2]

Brenda recalls that from this *'desperately, unpromising situation'* as a crippled child in-patient at Hartshill, she was first introduced to the delights of Trentham Gardens. With no National Health Service in those days, money was at a premium and had to be literally 'wrung' out of the public, particularly wealthy businessmen. There was a constant stream of fund raising events to not only keep the hospital going, but also to provide little treats for the children. For example, at Christmas there was Santa Claus and presents, clowns, entertainers and carol singing with the children lying *'captured'* in plaster on their backs but, according to Brenda, *'enjoying every moment!'*

Then came summer with the trips to Trentham Gardens. For these, Brenda adds, the hard-working fund-raisers *'pulled out all the stops, not only with begging bowls,but also appealing for material and physical help.'* All forms of transport were freely volunteered by their owners to convey the children to Trentham - cars, vans, lorries and coaches. In addition, all the hospital staff were augmented with willing help from local boy scouts, girl guides, boys' brigade, and just about anyone else, to facilitate the movement of patients from the vehicles to lie or sit under Trentham's trees. It was one almighty effort, she emphasised, which brought immeasurable delight to the hospital-bound children like herself.

Having been lovingly and carefully transported to journey's end, blankets were spread over the chosen area of ground where the stretchers were placed under the summer laden trees. *'Can you imagine my feelings,'* she asks *'after lying in a hospital bed for twelve months, and having been transported on a warm, balmy summer's day to lie on a green grass bed and gaze up into the blue sky and watch the playful sun through the lattice of fluttering leaves?'* From her vantage point, she continued, *'the trees were e-n-o-r-mous(sic), the sun magical and the sky heavenly'.* It is all *'indelibly etched on my mind, even to this day.'* *'Think of the pleasure'* she said, *'given to those children through the immense generosity of everyone concerned including, of course, the Duchess, who gave all the facilities free of charge for the day, together with the use of her staff.'*

Brenda considers herself most fortunate that *'through clever medical attention',* she achieved *'a most successful cure by the time I reached my early teens.'* Later, she ballroom danced *'like a good 'un'',* and attended all the 'big band' events at the Trentham Gardens Ballroom she was able to, being *'so enamoured by the surroundings'.* In addition, she would arrive there each Sunday for the afternoon tea dance in the *'enchanting'* ballroom, partake of a meal around 5 - 6pm., and then stay on for the evening session. Whilst also being a regular visitor to Trentham's open air swimming baths, she never learned to swim, but freely admits to *'struttin' her stuff'* around the pool in the pre- and early war period. As a consequence, she maintains that her time at Trentham has always been *'happy, exciting and exhilarating.'* However, she remains eternally grateful for the dedication of the medical people of the time - *'I was certainly a lucky girl'* she says.

From such unpromising beginnings, Brenda seems to have acquired, and retained, an incredible zest for life, and a strong sense of self. Not surprisingly, this remarkable lady also retains *'a love of Trentham Gardens'* and she particularly savours those *'sweet and joyful moments'* of her younger days - *'salad days - green and beautiful'.*

But she has mixed recollections of Trentham from her first ever visit as a crippled child to her adult years of *'hours spent in happiness, both lively and peaceful.'* *'I seemed to gravitate towards its when in need of boisterous pursuits, or with maturing years realising the beauty of its landscape, through to fully fledged adulthood, often calling on its calming influence when I yearned for solace and peaceful contemplation.'* *'All its charm in every season soothed my needs, the exhilarating springs, warm hazy summers, the enchanting autumns with the delight of shuffling through the multi-coloured carpet of fallen leaves, and the cold crisp incredibly magical winters.'* She considers herself fortunate to have had this *'haven of beauty to which she could escape'.* *'There were times when they restored my soul and gave me great courage to carry on. They were a tonic in more ways than one.'*

NOTES

1. *Millicent, Duchess of Sutherland and the Potteries & Newcastle Cripples' Guild.*
   D. W. Adams (Staffordshire County Library publication 1978) p 5
2. Ibid. p11

Brenda, 2nd right, and a girlfriend, in the company of two former Polish soldiers,
seen at a function in the Trentham Gardens Ballroom, 1951/52.

At Trentham Gardens around 1949. Head joiner,
William Barnett - June's grandfather - seen in his
workshop on the estate. *Courtesy Mrs J. Tooth*

June and friend on Captain, one of the Trentham Estate's
gentle giants.   *Courtesy Mrs J. Tooth*

Bill Barnett in the Control Room of the Trentham
Gardens Ballroom.   *Courtesy Mrs J. Tooth*

June and sister Christine at the entrance to Trentham
Park, during WWII.   *Courtesy Mrs J. Tooth*

14. JUNE'S GARDEN

Few readers can claim to have been born and raised on a thousand acre estate with gardens, woodland, a lake 1.5 miles in length, and an Art Deco style 130ft x 60ft swimming pool, but that was the experience of June Barnett (now Mrs Tooth). Born in 1935 on the Trentham Estate, this vast area became her informal playground and as she grew up it is not perhaps surprising that she came to regard it as *'her garden'*. In those seemingly far off days the situation was almost idyllic.

June's father was the estate's long-serving, highly respected electrician and the family lived in one of the tied residences of the mews type development situated on Park Drive, Trentham (this in recent years has been converted to luxury private apartments). Bill Barnett's 'empire' included the famous Trentham Gardens ballroom and during World War II, when the London Banks were evacuated to the premises, he was exempt military service as his knowledge and expertise were required to provide the electrical services essential to the Central Clearing House, as the finance centre became known. June's grandfather also lived in a bungalow on Park Drive, having served the Duke of Sutherland as Head Joiner. He was employed there when Trentham Hall was demolished in 1912.

June's early schooldays were spent at the nearby Trentham Church of England School on the A34 Stone Road. The headmaster was Mr Mellor who had a wooden leg. June recalls that as in the case of Long John Silver, you could hear him approaching and at times this filled the pupils with trepidation!

After school she happily returned to her domain. Frequently, she and her younger sister Christine would place the family's three cats in a doll's pram and they would wander into Spring Valley or another part of the woodland to play. As she grew up she learned to appreciate the local wildlife, no doubt encouraged by the estate's gamekeeper, James Hicks, and his staff. She has fond memories of helping Mr Hicks feed the deer and transporting the hay. As the years went by, life seemed so full for her as a teenager she recalled, *'there was always something going on, the Girls' Friendly Society, Girl Guides, the tennis club and riding lessons at Dimmock's Riding School on Longton Road'*. Her fondness for horses grew and whilst she did not ride on the estate itself, she spent as much time as possible with Trentham's *'gentle giants'* - the huge shire horses that worked there. She formed a particular *'friendship with Captain'* who was one of the team. She would hurry home from school to escort him to his field as the day's work on the estate came to a close.

Nowadays she has stopped riding, but she nevertheless continues to be involved with horses, passing on the skills to her young grand-niece.

June remembers the winters of the early 1940s with their heavy snow and the sight of skaters on Trentham Lake, giving the estate an almost Alpine atmosphere. Her grandfather had the responsibility of ensuring that the ice was safe for skating, and this initially involved drilling to determine its thickness. As a young girl June accompanied her grandfather as he checked that the ice was a minimum of 9 inches in depth before anyone was allowed onto its surface. She remembers that there were some really good skaters at the time, local residents and Bank personnel from the Central Clearing House. Others, not to be left out of the proceedings, used to deploy fold up seats from around the bandstand to push each other across the icy surface of the lake!

In 1945 No.164 Officer Cadet Training Unit (OCTU) was transferred to Trentham Park from Barmouth. This was one of a number of infantry training units whose successful cadets were eventually commissioned into infantry regiments. Whilst the units had been very much a wartime venture designed to 'churn out' officers (or 'cannon fodder' as one cadet remarked), young officers nevertheless remained much in demand to replace those being demobilised. The relocation of 164 OCTU also resulted in the arrival at Trentham of a number of military tailors, including a branch of the famous Moss Bros company of Convent Garden. There are those even today who can recall seeing signs in the vicinity advertising the various firms with the caption 'officers' uniforms made to order'.

The Moss Bros branch was surprisingly located in the front room of the Barnett household! Here they actually made and fitted the military uniforms for clients. The room was full of tailoring equipment - machines, rolls of material, boxes of military uniform accessories such as badges and officers' shoulder pips, not forgetting the customary full length tailor's mirror. The Barnett's hallway also had a full length mirror and June has enduring memories of seeing officer cadets being fitted out in their uniforms for passing out ceremonies at the camp in Trentham Park. 'They looked so smart with their badges and pips gleaming, and the polished leather Sam Brown belts'. 'Our property was so large that the two tailors lodged with us'. Whilst at Trentham the tailors made a suit for her father of which he was very proud, and they also supplied June with her first pair of jodhpurs - 'I felt like a million dollars'.

As electrician to the estate, Bill Barnett came into contact with famous bandleaders and personalities who appeared at the famous Trentham Gardens ballroom. It was his responsibility to ensure that spotlights, microphones and associated sound systems were installed as required and according to Percy Le Rolland, who played with both the Norman Jones and Ken Jones orchestras, 'Bill was a marvellous electrician'. June openly admits to taking advantage of the situation at times and 'pestering' her father to obtain autographs of visiting stars and to this day naturally treasures her collection which includes Joe Loss and the Beatles.

Bill Barnett's main hobby was beekeeping, his hives situated on land which is now used as the church car park. His reputation was such that he was regarded as an authority and would often lecture on the subject. He also frequently responded to calls to remove swarms from local residences.

June says proudly that her father was very versatile, also being a gifted craftsman who could make furniture, and a talented photographer. He received a long service award from the Countess of Sutherland in 1964.

June continued to live at Park Drive until she married in 1956 but she revisits her old haunts as often as possible.

Bill Barnett's beehives on the land off Park Drive, Trentham. *Courtesy Mrs J. Tooth*

Skaters on Trentham lake during World War II, photographed by a member of the Central Clearing House staff. *Courtesy Mrs Wildig.*

Trentham Gardens under heavy snow during WWII. Photographed by a member of the
Central Clearing House staff. *Courtesy Mrs Wildig.*

An 'alpine' scene at Trentham after a heavy snowfall during WWII, photographed by a member of the
Central Clearing House staff. *Courtesy Mrs Wildig.*

15. ACES & ERKS AT THE INSTITUTE

The former black and white pseudo-Elizabethan Village Institute at Trentham was used for various activities during its lifetime. No doubt this was the intention of its benefactor, the 4th Duke of Sutherland. Erected in 1894 on what is now the A34 Stone Road, its facilities variously included a billiard room, a stocked library, reading and classrooms, a kitchen and refreshment bar, and a workshop for handicrafts, together with quarters for a tenant caretaker. In later years it was also used as the local Girl Guide HQ.

However, it is not generally appreciated that prior to World War II the premises were also an important Royal Air Force Volunteer Reserve Training Centre. According to Vic Reynolds, Secretary of the North Staffordshire Branch of the Aircrew Association, the Centre was typical of a number set up in towns and cities throughout the country as war clouds gathered. The primary purpose of the RAFVR units was to produce a pool of men who, when qualified, could then be posted to RAF squadrons. All were volunteers (not conscripts) and when war was declared on 3rd September 1939 they were classed as mobilised. Considered important enough to have a Wing Commander as Commanding Officer, contemporary records show that nearly 200 personnel were under training at Trentham early in 1939. These included 20 pilots, 64 wireless operators/air gunners, 10 observers, and 100 ground staff. They were not all present in the building at one time, but divided into squads and required to attend at certain times on designated days. For example, those undergoing ground crew training were divided into five squads and reported on Thursdays or Saturdays, or as ordered. Special buses from various points around the city conveyed personnel into Trentham as required.

Vic was among the trainee wireless operator/air gunners at this time, and recalls that on entering the building, there were offices on either side of the corridor occupied by the CO, Adjutant and administration staff. The corridor opened out onto a main hall with classrooms and toilet facilities off. Outside at the rear, there was a small additional building of a similar style, together with a tower which was used to teach the basics of parachute jumping.

Vic's three month course at Trentham included the principles of navigation, map reading, morse code, and other skills essential to aircrew duties. On qualifying, and posting to their RAF squadrons, they received their uniform and kit, and were introduced to the delights of 'square bashing' before receiving further training relevant to their particular trade. Trainee pilots at such centres as Trentham were generally recruited from those who had had some private flying experience or from University Air Squadrons, and their training locally was linked with the nearby Meir Aerodrome which the RAF was then using as No. 28 Elementary and Reserve Flying School with Tiger Moth and Hawker Hart aircraft. Shortly after war commenced, the unit expanded to become No.1 Flying Practice Unit (FPU).

The unit was intended to be the first of its kind (the only one as it turned out) formed to accommodate 120 Acting Pilot Officers and 120 Sergeant Pilots who had completed advanced flying courses. As it happened, problems arose with billeting which resulted in the requisitioning of 3 large properties in the vicinity for the officers, and the housing of the NCO pilots in Longton Town Hall.

No. 1 FPU used Hawker Hind and Hector aircraft for training. The threat of invasion in 1940 had widespread effect, even at Meir, which by now was camouflaged. Arrangements were made for defence against parachutists and troop carrying aircraft, and regular exercises were held to ensure that all of the unit's 40 Hinds and Hectors could be dispersed around the perimeter within 15 minutes! Later that same year, the unit was disbanded and replaced by No. 5 Elementary Flying Training School which was transferred from Harwich in Middlesex. No. 1 FPU's aircraft were rapidly ferried away and replaced by Miles Magisters which became a familiar sight in the area.

It is worthy of note that a number of Vic's former Trentham RAFVR colleagues went on to have distinguished service careers. Among them Wireless Operator/Air Gunner Alec McEwen was awarded the DFC. Another W.Op/Air Gunner John Waite who together with Vic joined Coastal Command, was awarded the George Medal after rescuing 2 badly injured colleagues from a burning aircraft. Possibly the most famous Trentham trainee was John Ashton who became a distinguished flying ace and who played a prominent role in the Battle of Britain. Eventually attaining the rank of Wing Commander, he is credited with shooting down nine German aircraft. According to Vic, aircrews then consisted of a very large proportion of Voluntary Reserve personnel. Regulars were only a small percentage, and many of these were lost in the early period of the war, even before the Battle of Britain.

As the war progressed the Trentham RAFVR Centre continued to be used for administration and ground crew training, maintaining its links with Meir, but after hostilities ceased the Institute was utilised to accommodate No. 3509 Fighter Control Unit (FCU). Here, Royal Air Force Auxiliary personnel were trained in the use of radar, a number then progressing to early warning stations such as Hack Green in Cheshire and Fylingdale in Yorkshire. No. 3509 FCU not only trained them to monitor the skies, but also to direct fighter aircraft to respond in the likely attack from enemy counterparts. Vic recalled that this was a period when Britain was *'bang in the middle of a Cold War'* - *'a real threat!'*

The RAF finally left Trentham in the 1950s and the Institute was demolished in 1956. According to the late Geoff Cook, the building with its distinctive ventilation dome was *'in a perfect state of repair'* at the time of its demise. There are those even today who still regret the loss of the Insititute which was, after all, considered to be an important part of the area's heritage.

Trentham RAFVR flew out of Meir Airport using Tiger Moths. The airport had significant hopes of becoming a regional airport between 1930 and 1960. It is now a retail park.

The former Institute, Stone Road.
Photograph in the early 20th century by M.A. Head.

Vic Reynolds, taken in 1940.

BELOW:
Former Trentham RAFVR trainees taken at a reunion in the Holden
Bridge Hotel, Sneyd Green. 1985
L- R: Len Lewis, John F. Waite GM, Vic Reynolds,
Joe Holloway and Alec McEwen DFC

The Central Clearing House for the national banks was evacuated from London to Trentham on 26th August 1939, just before the onset of the Second World War.

Female staff are seen working here in obviously chilly conditions.

Potteries Museum

September 1941. CCH staff at Trentham Gardens Pool on the far side of the lake. *Lady Bryan collection*

Post Office and Paymaster General's section, Central Clearing House. It was in the Foyer. *Potteries Museum*

The Ballroom Bank, Central Clearing House at Trentham, 1939. *APACS.*

French sailors seen at Trentham Park in the 1940s. Around 5000 servicemen, the majority Free French, were encamped at Trentham Park from May to September 1940. They were visited on 25th August 1940 by George VI and General De Gaulle.
Evening Sentinel

Below: No 122 Military Convalescent Depot, with 1700 beds, was in Trentham Park from March 1943.
A party of convalesents are seen marching to a PT class February 1944.
Courtesy E.G.Bull

Between November 1945 and June 1946, 164 Officer Cadet Training Unit was based at Trentham Park, with around 800 personnel. RIGHT: Passing out parade, 9th March 1946.
Bebbington collection

For a short period in 1946 a Polish Resettlement Corps was also at Trentham Park before moving onto Blackshaw Moor near Leek.

In September 1947 all requisitioned Trentham Estates were reinstated.

16. TRENTHAM WARTIME PUBLICATIONS

World War II created a number of problems for newspaper proprietors, such as the introduction of censorship. Newsprint was a scarce and expensive commodity, and there was a constant need to maintain supplies. Stocks also had to be conserved against the threat of enemy bombing, and in the case of the local *Evening Sentinel*, they were stored in various unlikely locations in the district. Moreover, restrictions reduced the size of the newspaper by degrees to four pages per night, and sales were pegged to pre-war circulation figures. Certain editions were also discontinued. Given this situation, it is then perhaps surprising to learn of a number of new publications which originated from Trentham during this period, the circumstances arising entirely from the war.

The first publication was *The Outcast*, a house magazine for the staff of the London Clearing Banks - the Central Clearing House (CCH) who had been evacuated to Trentham Gardens Ballroom from the capital for the duration. Launched in February 1940, the publication's stated objective was defined as being to '*chronicle and entertain those who, by the exigency of war, found themselves in strange surroundings to carry on a vital national service.*'[1] The magazine was published regularly, initially under the joint editorship of Percy Woodruff and John Chater, featuring news and events relating to the CCH, whilst coincidentally attempting to entertain with contributions from the staff. Subsequently, it was to provide a valuable additional service in giving news of former colleagues who had been called to the colours. Printed locally by C. H. Vyse Ltd, the magazine ceased publication in 1943 due to '*pressure of changing*

conditions and personnel in the House'. Nonetheless, the then Comptroller of the establishment, Brian H. Bennett, expressed a wish that the magazine should continue in some form so as to *'present staff with a record of their activities and, at the same time, preserve a link with the past.'*[2] The result was the *Outcast Observer*, an 8 page monthly, its last edition coinciding with the closure of the CCH in June 1946. Unlike its predecessor, few copies of this publication appear to have survived.

In June 1940 Trentham Park became the temporary home of thousands of French servicemen following the fall of France.[3] The majority of these comprised survivors of the 13th Foreign Legion half brigade - 13th DBLE (demi-Brigade de la Légion Etrangère) and that of a half brigade of the Chasseurs Alpins (Mountain Light Infantry) . The sheer scale of operation in organising the vast camp presented many problems, not least communication. Within a short time, a climate of uneasiness began to develop, the population having increased to 5,530. Bewildered by events in France and confused about their status few, if any, were able to grasp a fundamental understanding of the situation. Nothing was initially known of the terms of the armistice, and the majority tended to believe that the war was over. In addition, a number of units had lost their officers and NCOs. This lack of leadership made liaison and communication extremely difficult.

The fact that a tense atmosphere was developing had also been observed by George Wigg (1900-1983), later Lord Wigg, on the occasion he visited the French camp on 24th June. At this period, Wigg was Secretary of the Workers' Educational Association and was living nearby at 117 Newcastle Road, Trent Vale. In association with A.D. Lindsay (later Lord Lindsay), Master of Balliol College, Oxford, he had been active in developing educational facilities in H.M. Forces. He organised a considerable number of lectures for the army units stationed in North Staffordshire, and he felt that the problem of morale of the French troops was one that might be usefully undertaken by him. After conferring with Ministry of Information officials, a number of measures were agreed, including the introduction of a camp newspaper.[4] The result was the daily *Journal du Camp* for *'information and entertainment'* and *'all the news will be given in a completely objective manner.'*[5]

Reading copies today, it appears that a genuine attempt was made to give the French troops information that would inform and interest them. On the other hand, some might argue that the 'selective' nature of extracts from the British press was, in itself, a form of censorship. An official of the Ministry of Information by the name of Kingsbury became responsible for the task of producing the newspaper, and he was assisted by a French NCO. Initially, printing was undertaken by the locally based Michelin Tyre Company before *The Times* newspaper assumed responsibility.[6]

In November 1945 yet a further friendly invasion occurred at Trentham Park with the arrival of No. 164 Officer Cadet Training Unit (OCTU) from Barmouth. This was one of a small number of infantry training units whose successful cadets were eventually commissioned into infantry regiments. The units had been very much a special wartime venture designed to churn out officers in an intensive 16 week course. However, despite peace having been restored and the victory celebrations over, young officers remained very much in demand to replace those rapidly being demobilised from the services. Under the command of Lt. Colonel D.L. Darling DSO, MC, the establishment comprised 5 companies - A, B, C,

D and HQ, the latter being responsible for training and administration. The training companies consisted of approximately 140 men, divided into platoons.

The OCTU produced its own newspaper, the *Trentham Times*, proudly emblazoned with the slogan - *'The only OCTU to own a newspaper!'* In addition, the training units published their own individual journals or house magazines with such titles as

The fire-watching team of the Barclays Bank contingent at CCH.

Courtesy of Sir Arthur Bryan

Clang and *Passing Fare*. The publications featured reports on activities in the fields of work, sports and social spheres, together with jokes, cartoons and other contributions from the officers and cadets. Some of these publications provide evidence of firms who especially moved into Trentham during this period. For example, advertisements show a number of military tailors in the area, three of whom were in premises on Park Drive. They were famous names, and they promised to provide *'uniform and equipment at its best with detail passing the Adjutant's eagle scrutiny.'* Another advert from a photographer offers *'special consideration to officer cadets.'*[7] Few examples of the OCTU publications appear to have survived.

A number of the Trentham publications, particularly *The Outcast*, also feature evidence of contributors' reactions to being evacuated to the area. Generally, North Staffordshire made favourable impressions on the CCH staff, who were impressed by the warmth of welcome from local residents. The ranks of the cadets at 164 OCTU contained a number of Dutch servicemen. Contemporary publications reveal that they, in particular, *'loved being here'* and enjoyed the *'excitement of training, the kindness of the people and the beauty of the countryside.'*[8]

The surviving Trentham publications provide a valuable insight into what life was like during a unique period of North Staffordshire's history, as seen by those who witnessed it and were part of it.

NOTES

1. The Outcast March 1940 p27
2. Ibid Vol III p365
3. Graham Bebbington, *Trentham At War* (Churnet Valley Books) Chapter 5
4. George Wigg. Memorandum to War Office ('French troops stationed at Trentham Park') July 1940 (undated).
5. Journal du Camp 27 June 1940
6. George Wigg. op.cit
7. *Trentham Times* Fifth edition (undated)
8. Jan Van Luyk 'Thanksgiving' in Passing Fare March 1946 p16

The great flood showing
Trentham Gardens under
water in October 1945.
Courtesy Mrs J. Tooth

Flooding behind properties on the
A34 Stone Road in the 1970s,
and below work in progress to
realign the River Trent to prevent
flooding in the 1980s.
Courtesy Mrs Joan Eaton

17. THE GREAT FLOOD OF '45

The British are famous for their obsession with the weather, and many will admit to always complaining about conditions, whether hot or sunny, or cold and frosty. At times, however, there have been natural catastrophes which produced conditions which the public have been justified in complaining about, irrespective of whether anything could be done to improve them.

For example, on 15th August 1953 a devastating North Sea surge inundated large areas of eastern England resulting in the loss of 307 lives and the evacuation of 30,000 people from their homes. Likewise, on 5th September 1958 a storm at Horsham in Sussex produced hailstones the size of small tennis balls, one of which was found to weigh 141 grams. Many also recall the blizzards which were a feature of the 1947 and 1963 winters. In both winters the south west of England endured the worst storms and in 1963 drifts of 25 ft deep were recorded at Princetown on Dartmoor where some were trapped in their homes for 8 weeks!

Locally, before improvements were made to the water course in the 1980s, the River Trent was prone to flooding on occasion at Hanford roundabout. The water would surge over the highway, flooding the former allotment site where the A34/A500 slipway is now situated, and the garage forecourt opposite. Also, at the rear of properties on the length of the northbound A34 Stone Road between Hissey's Turbine Garage and Hanford roundabout, the river would frequently burst its banks in storm conditions, flooding the fields on either side and giving the appearance of a huge lake.

In October 1945, the county's newspapers described Britain as being swept by *'great gales'* with the coasts being pounded by *'mountainous seas, ships in distress, winds of gale force and heavy rain locally.'* Torrential rain over a wide area of the Midlands was reported which resulted in heavy floods and considerable damage. The weekly *Staffordshire Chronicle,* with the headline *'heaviest floods for years',* described the river at Stafford as being at its highest for 6 years, with extensive flooding to certain properties including the town's cinema and Midland Red bus company garage. Similarly, the *Sentinel* in its editions of 28th & 29th October informed readers of *'the North Sea deluge'* and *'the area has its full share of the complex depression which has produced almost uninterrupted rain following nearly a week of gales.'* Many motorists were stranded, according to the newspaper, and trains delayed. The rain wreaked havoc in the area with extensive flooding resulting in *'3.88 inches in 9 days - one of the heaviest October deluges the district has experienced for many years.'*

Living in the mews type development in Park Drive on the Trentham Estate at the time, Mrs June Tooth found that she was unable to walk up the road to catch the bus to go to school in Stone. *'The area was one mass of water from the nearby Parish Church steps to our front door'* she recalls. The situation was exacerbated when the pools above the waterfall, situated near the Trentham Park Golf Course clubhouse, burst their banks. June remembers water, the colour of sand, surging down both the watercourse and the clubhouse access road, and then swirling around in the estate courtyard to a depth of 3-4 ft. Her father had a number of bee hives on an allotment site on the opposite side of Park Drive, and these were washed downstream and lost. A short distance upstream, at Hissey's Turbine Garage, a herd of pigs was drowned. The late Mrs Letty Hissey recalled the garden and surrounding area being *'completely flooded'* and *'leaving a real slimy mess when the water subsided!'*

At this time the Trentham Ballroom remained occupied by the London Clearing Banks (ie the Central Clearing House) which had been evacuated from the capital in 1939 for the duration. Ron Whittaker was one of the last of the local personnel to be employed there before it finally ceased operation and returned to London. He recalled sealed boxes of Recordak negatives (copies of cheques) from the CCH floating in the courtyard and having to be rescued by boat. The metal boxes had been stored in the stable block but as far as he is aware, the negatives were not damaged. It is believed that the boats used to retrieve the boxes were the property of HMS Daedalus II - a Royal Navy Artificer Training Establishment based at Clayton Hall during World War II. The boats, known as whalers, were stored at Trentham and regularly used for training purposes by the Fleet Air Arm apprentices from the training establishment.

Mrs Hazel Jenks remembers the flooding and the resultant death of an employee from the CCH. He is understood to have fallen from the bridge opposite the ballroom whilst attempting to take a photograph. His body was eventually recovered downstream at Strongford. Mrs Jenks says *'it was so deep it was impossible to define where the Italian Gardens ended and the lake began!'*

In the last century local weather statistics were maintained for many years by Ray Arundel, and these were regularly featured in the *Sentinel*. On 29th October 1945 that edition of the newspaper quoted Mr Arundel's records as showing that during the previous 10 days, the southern end of the city had received a total of 5.07 inches of rain. When I drew this to the attention of Mike Edge of Keele Weather Station in November 2003, he described the figure as 'incredible' and, having checked his data, confirmed that it was a record which remains unbroken.

Trentham Gardens under heavy flooding October 1945. Photographed by Ron Whittaker, one of the last locals to be employed by the Central Clearing House.

18. TRENTHAM'S HOLLYWOOD-STYLE LIDO

Already a major pleasure and entertainment centre in the 1930s, the owners of the Trentham Estate decided to supplement the successful ballroom. In 1935 an open air swimming pool was constructed on an area where a stream from Spring Valley entered the lake on its south western side. A contemporary brochure described the facility as having been provided *'with commendable care ....sited so as not to disturb the peace and elegance of the gardens themselves.'*[1] Nevertheless, some locals contended that construction works destroyed the former attractive entrance to the valley.

The pool was sheltered on three sides, forming a protective crescent from the wind on cool days. On two sides were massive oaks, with a belt of tall and stately pines on the third. The pool was described by a contemporary journalist as *'designed to harmonise with the natural beauty of the surroundings',* with the modernistic character of the building in light cream concrete *'fitting in admirably with the brightness of the setting.'*[2] The architect was Harold Goldstraw ARIBA.

There were many special features in the design of the pool. Foremost was the supply of water, construction allowing advantage to be taken of the natural springs of pure water issuing from the Hunter gravel beds. From the pool the water subsequently gravitated into the lake. In addition to its purity, the water was considered to contain certain medicinal qualities. After filtration to exclude any sand deposits, the water was raised to a temperature of between 60°-70° and there was a constant flow through the pool. Heating was by means of two low pressure boilers situated in the basement below the pool. There was a pump to recirculate the water when the pool was not in use by bathers.

The 132ft x 60ft pool was constructed in reinforced concrete, lined with polished concrete pre-cast blocks, and there was a painted concrete bottom inlaid with white tiles to denote the racing lanes. The shallow end was 3ft 3ins in depth, increasing to 8ft at the deep end. Here, a stainless steel chute was provided, together with spring boards and a 15ft high diving board. Further facilities included special lighting to transform the pool into *'a glistening sheet of loveliness by night'.* This was achieved by the arrangement underneath the water of 22 lighting pits containing floodlight reflectors which threw beams of light under the water for night bathing. The result was *'a marvellous sight at night.'* Around the pool area itself, teak seating was arranged for the benefit of spectators and bathers alike.

Access to the changing facilities was via an arched colonnade at the rear of the pool. A wide and imposing staircase gave access to an upper terrace where there was a large cafeteria with kitchen facilities. Sun blinds were fitted on the outside, and on either side of the building were terraces commanding excellent views of the pool and lake. A popular feature placed above the cafe, and recalled by many, was a mosaic-tiled clock with fish shaped fingers. Overlooking the pool was a cottage, in harmony with the other buildings, for use by the pool manager. Music could be provided to the pool area by means of a special sound system, incorporating loudspeakers hidden in the trees.

Although it was not officially open, the *Sentinel in* early July, 1935 reported that the pool was already attracting *'thousands of visitors ...everything points to it becoming the Mecca for the whole of the surrounding area.'* Opening times were advertised as 7am-10pm daily, with inclusive admission charges for spectators and bathers priced at 1s. 0d for adults, or 6d for children. Special floodlit bathing was to be held until 11pm every Saturday and Sunday.[3]

The opening ceremony was actually performed on 9th July 1935 before a large company of invited guests. In an introductory speech, his Grace the Duke of Sutherland said that he had always been a keen swimmer and knew from personal experience the great advantages swimming conferred on the health of the individual. *'If England is to be an A1 nation, it should encourage youth in outdoor sports such as swimming.'* He said that he was glad to note that North Staffordshire was in the forefront of swimming with such champions as Norman Wainwright and Bob Leivers. After congratulating all concerned on their work, the Duke announced his intention of donating a swimming trophy for competition amongst pupils of the district's secondary schools.

The pool was then officially opened by the Lord Mayor of Stoke-on-Trent (Alderman A.C. Harvey JP). More than 1,000 guests attended the afternoon ceremony, including those responsible for the design and construction of the scheme. After the official ceremony and a tour of the facilities by the chief guests, there followed a 'clever' display of swimming and diving by an exhibition team including Norman Wainwright and Bob Leivers. Subsequently, the Duchess of Sutherland presented gifts of souvenir pottery to the members of the display team. The celebrations continued into the evening, with guests being invited to the ballroom for dancing. Music was provided by Don Pedro & his Mexican Orchestra, supported by Rex & the Trentham Gardens Band. Members of the public were admitted from 8pm., the event ending at 11-45pm.[4]

In 1938 the long trek to the pool was made easier by the provision of a miniature railway. This not only served the pool, but continued along the complete length of the western side of the lake. This facility proved to be very popular, making it easier for families to reach the bathing area quickly, instead of walking the distance accompanied by small children and perhaps laden with picnic goods. At either end of the single track line, backs of seats would be reversed so that passengers were continually facing the direction in which the train was travelling. Simple as it may seem, the procedure to reverse one's own seat was regarded by some children as a great treat!

During World War II and the presence of the evacuated Central Clearing House from the capital, the pool was extremely popular with the staff who regularly organised inter-bank swimming matches or 'splashes.'[5] They also used the lake during the winter period for skating. The pool was also a popular venue for the Fleet Air Arm officers and apprentices from HMS Daedalus II based nearby at Clayton Hall. They were allowed free use of the facilities, and often parties would march down to Trentham from the training establishment. Daedalus maintained a number of cutters and whalers on the lake for training purposes.[6]

It is only to be expected that the pool was also popular with the children of the Trentham Estate families, even in the winter. Vera Hicks recalls walking from her home to the pool, taking a number of cushions. On arrival she would ascend the chute, sit on the cushions and slide down onto the ice and along to the end of the pool! Needless to say, the thickness had been tested for safety purposes before any of the children were allowed to venture onto the ice.

The Hollywood style pool was *'the most magnificent place that one could imagine'* according to Philip Bradbeer, Trentham's former General Manager. *'The magic of the place left a lasting impression ....it was wonderful, just like part of a Hollywood film set. I can't imagine another pool that came anywhere near it.'* The pool was generally open daily from Whitsun until the end of August, with attendances ranging from 20,000 -30,000 during a Bank Holiday weekend. During the 1950-60 period some families surviving on low wages would spend whole days by the pool, with modest picnics to satisfy their hungry offsprings. *'There was a tremendous atmosphere'* said Philip.

In later years, barbeques were regularly organised, sometimes in conjunction with The Place night club of Hanley. *'Drink was not a problem then'* said Philip, *'Perhaps people drank more sensibly, or could not afford too much anyway.'* Of course, like the famous ballroom, the pool was a much favoured venue for males seeking females, and vice versa.

The pool continued to be popular in later years, even being used for training hopefuls for the 1968 Olympic swimming team. However, by the 1970s it had possibly *'come to the end of its useful life'.* According to Philip Bradbeer there was evidence of mining subsidence at the pool and an amount of money was needed to repair it. In 1975 it was closed and later demolished during the period that the estate was in the ownership of the National Coal Board.

NOTES

1. Trentham Gardens brochure (undated).
2. *Sentinel* 4th July 1935
3. Ibid
4. *Sentinel* 10th July 1935 and Staffordshire Advertiser 13th July 1935
5. See *Trentham At War* (Churnet Valley Books) Graham Bebbington p67
6. See *Ship Without Water* (Churnet Valley Books) Graham Bebbington pp48 & 63

BELOW:
Trentham Gardens lakeside railway engine 'Dunrobin' with young enthusiast.
Courtesy Mrs G. Cook

The open air pool and the miniature railway seen in the 1960s.

Aerial view of the famous open air swimming pool, taken by Philip Bradbeer from a helicopter, early 1960s. The miniature railway can be seen to the right.

TRENTHAM SWIMMING POOL
New Amenity to Famous Gardens

In the front row are the Duke and Duchess of Sutherland, the Lord Mayor and Lady Mayoress of Stoke, and Mr. Goldstraw, the architect

Extract from The Staffordshire Advertiser, 13th July 1935.

**THE THREE PAGES THAT FOLLOW ARE A REPRODUCTION OF THE OFFICIAL
OPENING PROGRAMME FOR THE OPEN AIR SWIMMING POOL**

TRENTHAM SWIMMING POOL

ORDER OF PROCEEDINGS
9th July, 1935

2-50 The Duke and Duchess of Sutherland will arrive at the Swimming Pool, and will be received by Mr. F. Todd, the Resident Agent, Mr. E. P. Turner, M.I.Min.E., Engineer, Mr. E. Boudry, Manager, and Mr. R. Boudry, Deputy Manager of the Swimming Pool.

2-55 The Lord Mayor of Stoke-on-Trent (Ald. A. C. Harvey, J.P.), accompanied by the Lady Mayoress, together with Mr. T. H. Averill, Chairman of the Stone Rural District Council, will arrive at the Swimming Pool, where they will be received by His Grace The Duke of Sutherland and the Duchess of Sutherland at the main staircase.

3-10 The Chairman of the Stone Rural District Council will call upon Mr. Todd to present to the Lord Mayor and the Lady Mayoress, and to the Duke and Duchess of Sutherland, the following gentlemen, who have been responsible for the design and construction of the scheme:—
Mr. E. P. Turner, M.I.Min.E., Engineer
Mr. Harold Goldstraw, A.R.I.B.A., Architect
Mr. Peter Lind, Contractor
Mr. Jacobsen, Engineer-in-Charge
Mr. F. F. Plant, A.M.I.Mech.E., Assistant Engineer
Mr. Keepen, Foreman-in-Charge

3-15 The Lord Mayor and Lady Mayoress, accompanied by the Duke and Duchess of Sutherland, and the Chairman of the Stone Rural District Council, will then proceed to the Cafe Terrace, where the Chairman of the Stone Rural District Council will ask the Duke to make an introductory statement.

3-20 The Chairman of the Stone Rural District Council will ask the Lord Mayor of Stoke-on-Trent to formally declare the Swimming Pool open, following which the pennants will be hoisted.

3-25 Mr. Averill will then introduce the Vice-Chairman of the Trentham Pool Amateur Swimming Club (Mr. Spencer Stanway) to present to the Lord Mayor and Lady Mayoress and to the Duke and Duchess the following ladies and gentlemen taking part in the Display :

Mr. Norman Wainwright   Mr. Norman Brookes
Mr. R. H. Leivers   Mr. Tom Scott
Miss Edna Hughes   Mr. Walter Scott
Miss Nora Wall   Mr. Ernest Jones

3-30

DISPLAY *of* SWIMMING *and* DIVING

Under the auspices of the Trentham Pool Amateur Swimming Club,
affiliated to the Midland Counties Amateur Swimming Association, and the
Staffs. County Amateur Swimming Association

(UNDER A.S.A. LAWS)

Exhibition Swim of Four Lengths Crawl Stroke by Mr. Norman Wainwright
(Hanley A.S.C.) Champion of England. Olympic and International Swimmer

Exhibition Swim by Miss Edna Hughes
(Walsall A.S.C.) 100 yards Champion of England. Olympic and International Swimmer

Diving Display by Mr. Ernest Jones
(Newcastle A.S.C.) Champion Local Diver

Exhibition Swim, including the Crawl, Breast, and new Butterfly Stroke, by Mr. R. H. Leivers (Longton A.S.C.) 440 yards Champion of England. Olympic and International Swimmer

Mannequin Parade by Miss Mollie Shaw's Young Ladies, of Swimming Costumes, kindly provided by Messrs. Jantzen, through the Agency of Messrs. Henry White, Ltd., Newcastle, Staffs.

Surprise Item—Duggie Ascot, of London, the World's Worst Surfoplanist

Display of Fancy and Slow Motion Swimming by Miss Nora Wall
(Smethwick R.A.A.) Champion Swimmer of the Civil Service

Display of Speed Swimming by Mr. Norman Brookes
(Oldham Police A.S.C.) International Water Polo Player. Former Sprint Champion of England. Olympic and International Swimmer

Demonstration of Back Stroke Swimming by Mr. Norman Wainwright

Diving Display by Messrs. Tom and Walter Scott, International Divers

M.C. for Swimming : Mr. SPENCER STANWAY, President Staffs. A.S.A.

The Display is timed to finish at 4-40

4-25   The Lord Mayor and Lady Mayoress, together with the Duke and Duchess of Sutherland and party, will then be escorted by the Architect, Engineer, Resident Agent and Manager, on a tour of inspection of the buildings.

During this tour the display of swimming and diving will continue.

Ices and soft drinks will be served during the events.

4-40   The Duke of Sutherland will thank the Lord Mayor of Stoke-on-Trent for his attendance and for performing the opening ceremony, and the Chairman of the Stone Rural District Council for presiding.

4-45   The Duchess of Sutherland will present gifts of souvenir pottery to the Exhibition Swimmers.

5-0   At the conclusion of the Display guests are invited to return to the Entertainment Hall in the main Gardens for Thé Dansant, where Don Pedro and his Mexican Orchestra will be in attendance until 7-30 p.m.

Guests who wish to do so may remain for swimming, and will be provided with tea at the Swimming Pool Cafe.

The Pool will be available to the public at **6-30** p.m.

Don Pedro's Mexican Dance Orchestra, supported by Rex and his Trentham Gardens Band, will play for dancing in the Entertainment Hall from 8 pm (when the public will be admitted) terminating at **11-45** pm

The art deco pool was at the west side of the lake. Built in 1935 it was fed by natural springs.
It was closed in 1976 and cleared some 10 years later. Photo D.Brookes, Newcastle. *Courtesy Mary Bratby*

19. TRENTHAM SCHOOLDAYS

Looking back at her childhood and comparing it to some raised in the city, my wife Lynne maintains that her upbringing could perhaps be described as almost idyllic. She was raised in a loving family environment, in their home on the main road to Trentham. They were fortunate not only to have a long garden, but also fields behind the property which gently rose to Northwood Lane.

Through this area of open undulating countryside meandered the River Trent on its way south to the Trentham Estate. The fields were a constant paradise for her and Peter and David, her younger brothers - truly an informal adventure playground. Cows grazing in the fields would occasionally come and explore the family's garden if the gate had not been secured properly, and their dog loved to escape and chase the rabbits! Of course, they got up to mischievous pranks at times, but nothing bad, otherwise her parents would learn of it and act accordingly!

Lynne in the field behind her garden in Stone Road with Trentside Hotel in the background.

The distinguished artist Reginald Haggar and his wife lived on the opposite side of the road, and often he would be observed sitting in the fields with his easel and brushes painting views of the Trent Valley.

Lynne's early schooldays were spent at Trentham Church of England School on Stone Road. The black and white Victorian school building stood opposite the Monica Café (now the Poachers Cottage) in a small cluster of similarly designed buildings including The Institute. Sadly, none of these magnificent pseudo-Elizabethan style properties have survived. Outside the school building was a small playground situated to the left, where a toilet block was also located.

Lynne recollects pupils entering the seat of learning via an open porch on the front of the building. Here the crates of milk were delivered and stored until taken into the classrooms for distribution or, in the winter periods, for warming in the hearth. Entering the porch, a door opened onto a corridor to the right of which were two classrooms divided by large sliding doors. This was the infants' accommodation with the customary desks and also a rocking horse and sandpit. On the left of the main corridor was a further classroom for older children, a cloakroom with sinks and the head teacher's office. Even in the late 1950s, when Lynne attended, the school was lit by gas and heated by open fires, surrounded by fireguards.

Meals were not cooked on the premises, but delivered daily in stainless steel containers. The older children took their meals in the corridor, whilst the infants had theirs in the classroom.

At the time that Lynne attended the Head Teacher was Mr Faram, whilst the staff comprised Mrs Eagles, Mrs Massey and Miss Shaw (Infants), together with Mrs Astbury and Mrs Hill (Juniors).

Morning assembly commenced daily with the singing of Sullivan's setting of 'Onward Christian Soldiers' - it was the only music that the pianist could play! Being a small school it had no gymnasium facilities, and sporting activities, such as they were, including sports day, took place in the park.

Trentham Gardens railway station, the branch line of which closed in 1957, was within a short distance of the school. In the Spring and Summer, pupils were escorted on nature rambles along the track, the teachers taking the opportunity to point out the flora, fauna and wildlife. The former single line track had earlier been a popular facility for conveying passengers to Trentham Gardens, particularly at holiday periods, but it was particularly busy during World War II as a result of the London Clearing Banks being evacuated to the Gardens. The branch line was also used from time to time to accommodate the Royal Train, where it would park overnight under guard.

Lynne also remembers the school visitors including the 'Nit Nurse' and the school medical officer, Dr Dash, who undertook regular inspections of the pupils. On such occasions, pupils would line-up in the corridor and be individually taken behind a temporary screened-off area in the cloakroom to be examined. When the doctor came, a parent had to accompany the child during the examination.

In the property next to the school lived Mr Gouldstone, the driver of the popular Trentham Gardens lakeside steam engine, and his wife. He would often be seen setting off on his cycle to work in his oily overalls and cap. Naturally a number of the boys were envious of his position! Part of the schoolyard overlooked the rear of the Gouldstone's house, and their family cat was a popular attraction for the children as it often arrived at the back door with a mouse which it had caught on the railway line.

Being a Church of England School, there was a close association with the nearby St. Marys & All Saints Parish Church which abuts Trentham Gardens and the remains of its Hall. On the occasions that special services were held such as Christmas, Ascension Day and Harvest Festivals, all pupils would parade across to the Church where the proceedings would be conducted by the Rector, Rev. Ramsden. In turn, the kindly Rector often visited the school, but usually in his civvies. Ascension Day was very popular with the pupils because following the service the rest of the day was usually declared a holiday!

In 1960 celebrations were held to mark the 50th Anniversary of the uniting of the six towns to form the County Borough of Stoke-on-Trent. Participating in the event, Lynne remembers being taken into Trentham Park with her fellow pupils where they were each given a box containing sandwiches and cake, and presented with a commemorative mug.

The Monica Café could perhaps be regarded as an unofficial tuck shop as at lunch times and after school a number of pupils regularly visited the premises to purchase sweets. In this period

The former Monica Café on the Stone Road.
It has since been extended and is now known as The Poacher's Cottage. *Courtesy Mrs Barbara Hobson*

The A34 Stone Road at Trentham undergoing reconstruction to form the dual carriageway. Sadly, historic buildings to the right of the photo were lost during this period. *Bebbington collection*

The infant class of Trentham C of E School about 1957. Lynne Bebbington (née Eaton) is third from left, back row. Class teacher Mrs Eagles is on left.

the A34 was a single lane carriageway, not so busy as today, and consequently easier to cross. Nonetheless, the highway code was strictly observed!

A short time prior to closure of the school, Lynne and a number of her colleagues who lived within the City boundary were taken to Thistley Hough High School, Penkhull to sit the 11 plus examination. She distinctly remembers finding the large examination centre overwhelming and daunting. On the following morning those who had sat the exam were taken on a trip to the Blue John Cavern in Derbyshire. But for Lynne, the outstanding school trip was that on one of the last steam trains from Trentham main line station to London, to visit the Tower of London and Hampton Court - a day to remember!

In the 1960s, the area began to be developed with more housing and, to improve facilities for the additional children, both Trentham and Hanford Church of England Schools closed and were merged into the newly built Priory School. Lynne was attending Trentham School when it closed in 1962 and was thus transferred to the Priory before moving on again to Oakhill Junior High School.

It is perhaps fair to comment that Trentham School had become inadequate for the standard required at that time. It was incapable of being extended and its facilities were out of date. Nonetheless, Lynne believes that when it was demolished, together with the surrounding buildings, it was a sad loss to our heritage. Today, planning legislation may have made it more difficult to remove the properties and, if nothing else, they would have been a valuable tourist attraction.

Trentham School taken in 1965 by Mr G. Cook, just prior to demolition. The photo was taken from the site of the former Institute, with Mr. Gouldstone's house to the left. *Bebbington collection*

Adrienne Holtham at Trentham, backed by the Reg Bassett Band, about 1975. *Courtesy The Sentinel*

A Senior Service cigarettes sponsored concert in the ballroom in the early 1960s. *Courtesy Philip Bradbeer*

20. THE LAST WALTZ

Built in 1931, Trentham Gardens Ballroom was reputed to be one of the finest in the country. According to dance enthusiasts, it could hold its own against any similar venue, including Blackpool's famous Tower Ballroom. Dances attracted thousands from a wide area, and scores found their future partners there. With its 18,000 sq.ft of polished maplewood floor, the Trentham ballroom could accommodate 3,500 dancers, or 2,000 seating for concerts or conferences.[1] It was so large that during sequence dances, couples were likely to circle the hall only twice, or three times at the most. Likewise, when old time dances were taking place, they would be unlikely to progress around the room once! All agree that the atmosphere in the glittering ballroom was magic.

The ballroom's dancing period hey-day was undoubtedly the post war era. Then, the ladies wore cocktail dresses and the men dressed in collar and tie. Local bands in attendance included Reg Bassett, Ray Piper, Norman Jones, Wallace Sethna, Ken Griffiths and Ken Jones, and they also supported the famous big bands on their visits - Ronnie Aldrich & the Squadronnaires, Ted Heath, Nat Temple, Joe Loss, Johnny Dankworth, Ray McVay, Ivy Benson, and Geraldo who became Trentham's Director of Entertainment. Even the renowned Ray Conniff played at Trentham, an occasion which Philip Bradbeer, Trentham's former General Manager, remembers particularly. *'The American bandleader was a perfectionist ....personally checking each item of equipment himself before the performance. The result was that you heard that wonderful Ray Conniff sound, just as on record.'* For those with a preference for strict tempo, there were visits by Victor Sylvester and Sydney Thomson, whilst those with a latin disposition were catered for by no less than Edmundo Ros. Subsequently, with the advent of traditional jazz, devotees were entertained by the likes of Acker Bilk, Chris Barber and Kenny Ball.

In the 1960s and 1970s, with the emergence of pop groups, artistes included The Beatles, Gerry & the Pacemakers, The Big Three, The Who (Philip Bradbeer particularly remembers drummer Keith Moon arriving in his purple Rolls Royce), Emerson, Lake & Palmer, The Animals, Genesis, Led Zeppelin, Manfred Mann, and Tom Petty & the Heartbreakers. It is also interesting to note that in 1975, Status Quo recorded a number of tracks live during one of their appearances at Trentham. These were eventually issued on a Phonogram 45rpm EP.[2] By the 1960s, the mode of dress of Trentham patrons had been changed with the boys in drapes and winkle-picker shoes or brothel creepers, and the girls in swirling skirts, seamed nylons and stiletto heels! By the 1970s, men tended to have the long hair styles favoured by the groups, and the standard uniform for males and females alike was denim jackets and flared jeans.

In recalling the wonderful times they had in the ballroom, almost everyone spoken to mentions the acoustics and the amazing sounds of the bands. For this, credit should be given at least in part to Bill Barnett, Trentham's long serving chief electrician, who was responsible for the ballroom's mikes, sound system, spotlights etc. In particular, saxophonist Percy Le Rolland of the Ken Jones Orchestra paid tribute to Bill. But Percy observed that whilst the ballroom's sound system was good for that time, he freely admitted that today's was far superior. *'The ballroom was a vast place, and microphones were not placed on instruments like today.'* Consequently, the sidesmen learned a technique to *'throw the sound'* which filled the place in which they were playing.

Percy also recalls two amusing incidents which occurred during visits of the Ted Heath Band, one occasion being when popular vocalist Lita Roza was in attendance. Percy had purchased some flowers for his wife from a Trentham Gardens sale and he was carrying these across the empty ballroom to place with his instruments until he went home. As he approached the stage, Lita appeared from the side, and thinking the flowers were for her said *'how kind of you'* and took them. The other incident involved vocalist Paul Carpenter who rudely interrupted a conversation between Bill Barnett and some of the Ken Jones sidesmen. 'Who is Sparks?' he asked, to which Bill answered that he was. The singer declared, *'I want more spotlights on me!'* *'How many do you want?'* enquired Bill, to which Paul Carpenter responded *'Do you know who I am?'* The somewhat exasperated electrician countered *'I don't care who you are, that's all there is'.* According to Percy, the singer had no spotlight for the rest of his performance!

Adrienne Holtham (now Mrs Beech) sang with the Reg Bassett band in the 1970s. She was the daughter of the late local band leader, Arthur Holtham. Having 'graduated' from performing in youth club pantomines and chapel concerts (she was, on occasion, accompanied on the piano by the author!) she says that *'there is nothing to beat singing with the accompaniment of a big band ...there is nothing to compete with that wonderful backing behind you.'* Adrianne agreed that whilst the ballroom's sound equipment was very good for that period, it was not of the high standard as today. She too learned to develop a technique of *'throwing her voice',* just like the musicians *'threw the sound from their instruments'.* According to Philip Bradbeer, Adrianne was the youngest vocalist regularly appearing at the ballroom and she was very popular. Adrianne herself says she made friends with many of the regulars, and recalls *'the tremendous atmosphere',* particularly on New Years Eve with the build up to the chimes of Big Ben which were relayed over the loudspeakers at midnight.

Another popular vocalist at Trentham was Jackie Trent. Formerly Yvonne Burgess, the Chesterton born singer-songwriter is perhaps better known to younger audiences today as the co-writer of the theme to 'Neighbours', but in 1965 she had a No.1 hit with 'Where are you now my love?' Composed with her husband to be Tony Hatch for the Granada TV drama 'It's dark outside', the record unseated The Beatles' 'Ticket To Ride' from the lead position. She went on to co-write the musicals 'Rock Nativity' and 'The Card' with Tony, also having success with songs such as 'Joanna', 'Don't sleep in the subway' and 'I couldn't live without your love' which achieved almost classic status with Scott Walker and Petula Clark respectively.

Jackie's potential was spotted and appreciated at Trentham long before she achieved fame internationally. According to Percy Le Rolland - *'some have got it, some haven't - Jackie Trent had!'* Even then she was somewhat of a veteran, having been entertaining since she was 8 years old. She was very confident, and *'never backward at coming forward',* said Percy. *'Jackie was not likely to*

COME DANCING AT—

Trentham Gardens

TELEPHONE: 57341/3 STOKE-ON-TRENT, STAFFS.

THE LARGEST BALLROOM IN THE MIDLANDS
FULLY LICENSED ROMAN BAR

CHRISTMAS AND NEW YEAR ATTRACTIONS
1965/6

GET YOUR TICKETS EARLY !

CHRISTMAS EVE BALL

FRIDAY, DECEMBER 24th, 7-30—12 p.m. Tickets 10/6 each

TWO BAND FEATURE

Jack Kirkland & His Broadcasting Band
REG BASSETT & HIS BALLROOM ORCHESTRA

LICENSED BARS   LATE BUSES AS USUAL

CHRISTMAS OLD TIME BALL

TUESDAY, DECEMBER 28th, 7-30—12p.m. Tickets 7/6 each

WALLACE SETHNA AND HIS OLD TIME ORCHESTRA

M.C.'s HAROLD AND CHRIS LLOYD

FULLY LICENSED BARS

BOXING NIGHT BALL

MONDAY, DECEMBER 27th, 8p.m.-2a.m. Tickets 12/6 each

NON-STOP DANCING TO

Bob Miller & The Millermen
REG BASSETT & HIS BALLROOM ORCHESTRA
Jack Kirkland & His Broadcasting Band

LICENSED BARS   LATE BUSES AS USUAL

NEW YEARS EVE CARNIVAL BALL

FRIDAY, DECEMBER 31st, 8p.m.-2a.m. Tickets 20/- each

NON-STOP DANCING TO

Nat Temple & His Orchestra
REG BASSETT & HIS BALLROOM ORCHESTRA
Terry Gore & His Show Band

LICENSED BARS   LATE BUSES AS USUAL

* POPULAR SATURDAY DANCES *

* JACK KIRKLAND AND HIS BROADCASTING BAND *
* REG BASSETT AND HIS BALLROOM ORCHESTRA *

LICENSED BARS — HUGE CAR PARK — LATE BUSES
EARLIER DANCING 7-30 p.m.—12 p.m. ADMISSION 6/-

SPECIAL CHRISTMAS BINGO SESSION

"NATIONAL GOLDEN SCOOP" PLUS "£200 JACKPOT"
NUMEROUS XMAS PRIZES, XMAS HAMPERS, ETC.

SUNDAY, DECEMBER 19th. EYES DOWN 7-30 p.m., PROMPT. TICKETS 2/6 EACH (members only)

Tickets at the Main Gate or Ballroom Box Office, Trentham Gardens, Telephone
Stoke-on-Trent 57341, or the following agents—

BEVANS MUSIC SHOP, Stone, Tel. Stone 159; BLANEYS, 6 Merrial Street, Newcastle,
Tel. 65041; T. W. DAVIS (Longton) Ltd., 51 The Strand, Longton, Tel. 33380; RIDGWAYS,
80 Piccadilly, Hanley, Tel. 25062; SHERWINS, Market Square, Hanley, Tel. 21621; WAYTES,
3 Glebe Street, Stoke, Tel. 47755; WAYTES, 4 Commercial Street, Longton, Tel. 34552.

POSTAL BOOKING SLIP

To Manager, Trentham Gardens Ballroom, Stoke-on-Trent:

Please forward..............Tickets for...... ....Date...............

take any notice of protocol ...if a door was marked 'private', she would be likely to go through it!' Jackie is still entertaining and is on the International Board of the Variety Club of Great Britain.

Mrs Brenda Kitching has many fond memories of the ballroom. *'Just before hostilities commenced in 1939, the dances were happy go lucky carefree events, and very exciting for the local girls attending because boys travelled even then from Manchester, Birmingham, Stafford etc to congregate in the beautiful and lavishly equipped venue.'* She *'strutted her stuff with gusto'* to the big bands of the day and *'enjoyed every moment'*. *'New Years Eve dances in particular were so popular, one was lucky to procure a ticket.'* *'Midnight was a happy maelstrom of excitement with hooters, whistles, buzzers, balloons, paper streamers and hugs and kisses - what joy!'* She remembers at one of the *'memorable New Year bashes'* being quite upset to discover the loss of an ear-ring which was *'a hoop of glamorous diamente'*. She told her mother that she would inquire at Trentham in the hope of recovering it, but her mother ridiculed the idea as a wasted effort. But Brenda discovered the ear-ring had, in fact, been found amongst *'the heaving, celebrating mob'* and thanks to the honesty of some kind, unknown patron, she still has that treasured item of jewellery today!

In the post war period, Brenda discovered sad stories during otherwise pleasurable attendances at the ballroom. Among the male partners with whom she danced were many European refugees who were former members of their respective countries' armed services. They had fled to England to join the allied forces to help free their homelands, but now found themselves in tragic situations. *'Some had lost their homes and whole families, having to make a new life with very little or nothing to restart with.'* Brenda met *'highly educated, cultured people'* who had began to make a new living in the local mines or potbanks - *'they were so courageous and determined.'*

In particular, she remembered one Polish gentleman who started working in a potbank, thoroughly learned the trade and eventually succeeded in owning his own pottery company! In contrast, she met a *'courteous'* former Czechoslovakian pilot working at Norton Colliery who became *'a hopeless alcoholic'*. *'It really tugged at my heartstrings as I watched helplessly his sad decline from a gallant gentleman to a pitiful casualty of that terrible war.'*

Tony Gregory has fond memories of dancing to Geraldo's orchestra. He also spoke of the *'fantastic atmosphere of the New Years Eve dances, with the ballroom so packed, you could hardly move.'* *'Beer was served in large enamel jugs which saved time in journeys to the bar.'* *'Patrons were searched on arrival at one period',* he recalls, *'in a move to prevent spirits being imported onto the premises'.* Tony's solution was to leave it in the car and retrieve it later when he had obtained a pass!

Silverdale born Christine Ward (nee Mullineux) recalled regularly travelling from her home to Trentham by bus *'dressed up to the nines',* having joined up with friends en route. *'There was always a feeling of anticipated excitement each time you went to Trentham, something about the place as you walked through the doors, perhaps it was the big band sound.'* *'On arrival there was impatience to deposit your coat at the cloakroom before hurrying into the ballroom to find a table'.* She, like many others, retains particular memories of the special evenings such as Christmas Eve and New Years Eve with the balloons, streamers and glittering mirror globes adding to the atmosphere.

Trentham Gardens
AUGUST
ATTRACTIONS
AT THE MIDLANDS' GAYEST RENDEZVOUS

FULLY LICENSED ★ LATE BUSES

FRIDAY NIGHTS - TWO BAND ATTRACTIONS

FRIDAY AUGUST 7th
TOP OF THE POPS
THE ANIMALS

FRIDAY AUGUST 14th
The Popular Radio and T.V. Stars
THE BIG THREE

FRIDAY AUGUST 28th
Return visit of
KENNY BALL & HIS JAZZMEN

Supported by REG BASSETT and his ORCHESTRA
8 p.m. - 1 a.m. ★ LATE BUSES ★ TICKETS 6/6 Each ★ Usual Agents

---

THE POPULAR SATURDAY DANCE
EVERY SATURDAY
SELECT DANCING TO
KEN JONES and the Trentham Gardens Ballroom Orchestra
8p.m.-11.45p.m. Admission 5/- Late buses

FRIDAY AUGUST 21st
7 30 p.m. - 1 a.m.   Tickets 7/6
GRAND SUMMER BARBECUE
at Trentham Swimming Pool
Dancing to well-known groups
Swimming in the Heated Blue Pool
Delicious Refreshments
Ferry Service between the Main Gate
and the Swimming Pool
*This is the last Barbecue of the Season—
be sure to book your ticket early*

THURSDAY AUGUST 27th
8 p.m. - 12 p.m.
OLD TIME BALL
featuring
WALLACE SETHNA AND HIS OLD TIME ORCHESTRA
M.C.'s HAROLD & CHRIS LLOYD
Tickets 5/6 Each   Usual Agents

WRESTLING
Two big-time International Promotions in August
Tuesday 11th and Tuesday 25th at 8 p.m.
Buffet - Licensed Bars - Special Concessions for Party or
Block Bookings - Huge Car Park
Seats 10/- to 5/-   Be sure to book Early
WATCH LOCAL PRESS FOR FULL DETAILS OF THESE
WRESTLING SPECTACULARS!

BINGO
Join Trentham Bingo Club and try your luck in the Great
Trentham £200 Jackpot, coupled with the fabulous
National Golden Scoop
Every Sunday and Wednesday
Doors Open 7 p.m.   "Eyes Down" 8 p.m.   Membership FREE
Each member may bring one guest.

BOOK A TABLE in the wonderful NEW HIGHLAND RESTAURANT
DINNER DANCE EVERY THURSDAY AND SATURDAY from 8 p.m. - Dancing to the Alan Fisher Trio
Inclusive Ticket One Guinea or 'a la carte' menu at moderate prices.
Excellent Service - First Class Cuisine - Exquisite Surroundings
For immediate personal attention to your requirements Telephone Stoke-on-Trent 57341 Ext. 25.

FULLY LICENSED CATERING THROUGHOUT THE GARDENS - HUGE CAR PARKS - EXCELLENT BUS SERVICES
Tickets at the Main Gate or Ballroom Box Office, Trentham Gardens, Stoke-on-Trent 57341, or the following agents:—

BEVANS MUSIC SHOP, Stone. Tel: Stone 159. BLANEYS, 6, Merrial Street, Newcastle. Tel: 65041. T. W. DAVIS (Longton) Ltd., 51, The Strand, Longton. Tel: 33380. LEWIS'S TRAVEL BUREAU, Hanley. Tel: 22263. RIDGWAYS, 80, Piccadilly, Hanley. Tel: 25062. SHERWINS, Market Square, Hanley. Tel: 21621. WAYTES, 3, Glebe Street, Stoke. Tel: 47755. WAYTES, 4, Commercial Street, Longton. Tel: 34552.

Tickets also available from: Bostocks, Congleton; Don Everall, Wolverhampton; Greatrex, Stafford; Mr. Handley, Cellarhead, (Byrnes Moorland Garage), Leek Travel Bureau; Hollinshead Garage, Scholar Green; Jones Coachways, Market Drayton; Niddries Coaches, Middlewich; Robert Coaches, Crewe; Salopia Luxitours, Whitchurch and Nantwich.

Christine recollects that it was most important to apply for tickets early for those special occasions, sometimes in October, so as to avoid disappointment.

Like Christine, the majority of patrons did not own cars and travelled to Trentham by bus. She remembers the rows of single and double decker PMT vehicles waiting outside to convey dancers home after events had ended. The transport was highly organised, with an inspector on duty responsible for allocating seats on the coaches. The journey home could sometimes take an hour or more, with the bus having to do a tour of an area to drop passengers off.

The area adjoining the ballroom and to the right of the foyer was known as the Orangery, or Greenhouse. This fulfilled many useful functions from bar area and restaurant, to theatre auditorium during World War II. The ballroom was used as the Central Clearing House for the duration of the war, and the Orangery became a regular venue for the Siren Theatre where the bank employees occupied their leisure in dramatic productions, and giving pleasure to others. Works such as Noel Coward's *Fumed Oak* and Priestley's *Dangerous Corner* were performed under the direction of the energetic and talented Leonard Crainford (one of the 'Outcasts' as those evacuated from London called themselves) who later joined the Council for Encouragement of Music and the Arts (CEMA). During the intervals, teas were served in the lounge surrounding the auditorium, for which tables could be reserved. Seats for the performance were 1/3d, teas 9d, and the bar opened at the end of the show. The Siren Theatre was also a successful ambassador for the CCH as it toured with many of its performances, not only helping to boost morale during the dark days of the war, but also raising many thousands of pounds for local charities. When it gave its final performance at Trentham on 11th May 1946, an invited audience of 450 attended.[3]

In the early 1960s, the estate trustees decided to replace the Orangery wing in a move to improve facilities. The result was the popular Roman Bar. Access was gained through a spacious new foyer with lifts and twin staircases leading up to the Highland Suite where the colour scheme was based upon the Sutherland tartan. Graham Plimbley was employed as a joiner on the rebuilding work in 1963. However, he subsequently fulfilled another role by joining the band 'Sunset' which was resident in the Highland Suite, playing on Saturday evenings and at other functions. The band personnel comprised Ken Underhill (guitar), Mervyn Ange (bass guitar), Dave Freer (drums), Sharon Scott (vocals) and Graham on piano.

It was during this period that the drinks licensing arrangements at Trentham Gardens were to change. According to Philip Bradbeer, up to that point Joules of Stone had dealt with drinks licences, the brewers making applications as and when required. However, in 1962, the establishment was granted its own licence.

It is hard to imagine any similar venue having a greater diversification of use than the Trentham Gardens ballroom. In addition to being a first class dance hall where, on occasion, world class championship tournaments took place, other events included the likes of exhibitions, trade fairs, antique and craft fairs, fashion shows, flower shows, wrestling, boxing and snooker promotions, local university award ceremonies, computer and toy fairs etc. The ballroom was also the venue, at times,

*New Year's Eve
1982*

HIGHLAND SUITE, TRENTH

The Highland Room

Trentham Gardens

New Year's Eve Dinner Dance

Friday, 31st December, 1971

Tickets £ 4.50
NOT RETURNABLE

CHAMPAGNE COCKTAIL SERVED IN THE
GOLSPIE ROOM PRIOR TO
DINNER ONLY

THE OUTCASTS' DRAMA CLUB

*requests the pleasure of your
company at a*

FAREWELL PERFORMANCE

SATURDAY, 11th MAY, 1946

at 7-0 p.m.

at Siren Theatre, Trentham Gardens

Row   *B*   Seat No.   *8*

of the Annual Midlands Literary Lunch whose speakers included Lady Isabel Barnett, Ned Sherrin, Hammond Innes and John Braine. *'The diversification was absolutely fantastic,'* declared Philip Bradbeer. *'If I look back on my working life, whilst monetarywise it may not have been the best job in the world, the interest was there because day to day, week to week, we were dealing with different things, different people, stars, all sorts of events from the smallest to an international conference.'*

The festival season was not only popular at Trentham for its dances, but for the annual Christmas concert. The author and his wife have fond memories of the event when the ballroom would be full to seating capacity. The main attraction was the Royal Doulton Band, its members resplendent in their distinctive uniforms, and artistes

Graham Plimbley with American bandleader Les Brown, 1990.

usually included a vocalist(s). One year the guests included the Gnosall Handbell Ringers, their sound particularly adding to the atmosphere of the occasion. The ballroom at such times looked magnificent, highly festooned with decorations and with giant Christmas trees placed on the dance floor, either side of the stage. No expense appeared to have been spared. The music, of course, had a festive flavour and whilst the band and artistes fulfilled the major role, the audience were also given the opportunity to join in carols. The experience was not only a wonderful occasion with first class entertainment, but it was the event which we felt prepared us for Christmas.

Sadly, the magnificent ballroom is no more, but enthusiasts could not let its closure pass without marking the occasion. The unique event was a night of celebration and nostalgia and appropriately called 'The Last Waltz'. Organised by Norman Maddox and Harold Starkey, the event took place on 3rd August 2002 when many attended in period 1940s dress and danced to the Robert Shirley Orchestra. Attendance was reputed to be in excess of 1,000 and tickets were sold out within a short period of the date being announced on BBC Radio Stoke. Thankfully, the occasion has been well documented and filmed for prosperity by Professor Ray Johnson of Staffordshire University.[4] In the following year the complex was finally demolished as part of the £100m project now being undertaken by new owners, Trentham Leisure, to transform Trentham Gardens into *'a unique visitor attraction of national significance'.*

NOTES

1. Official figures quoted in Trentham Gardens brochure (undated).
2. The tracks featured on the Phonogram EP QUO13 are 'Roll over lay down', 'Gerdundula,' and 'Junior's wailing.' The author is indebted to Richard Durrant for this information.
3. Graham Bebbington, *Trentham At War* (Churnet Valley Books) p94.
4. Video *The Last Waltz* Staffordshire Film Archive.

An Interceramex exhibition in the ballroom in the 1960s. *Courtesy Philip Bradbeer*

Ken Dodd signing autographs at a trade promotion about 1965. *Courtesy Philip Bradbeer*

A dancing competition in the Ballroom in the 1960s.

The famous ballroom in the process of demolition. Photo by author 2003.

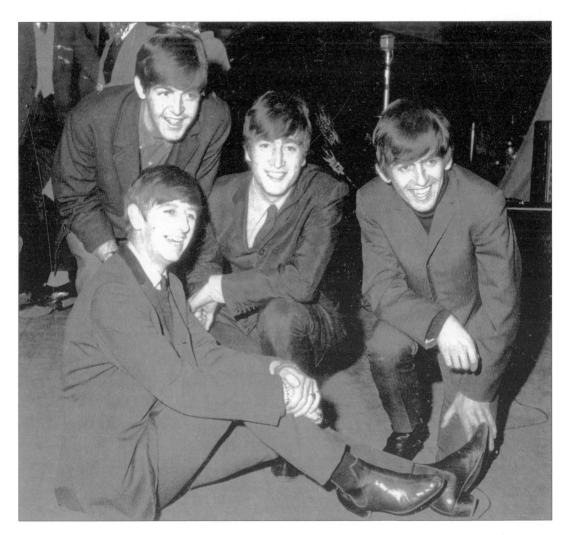

The Beatles relaxing after a gig, c 1963. *Courtesy Richard Durrant*

21. BEATLEMANIA AT THE GARDENS

The Beatles have become a part of everyday popular culture. It is difficult to comprehend that more than 30 years have lapsed since they split up as a group, yet interest in the 'Fab Four' remains remarkably high.

Their history has been well documented. Nevertheless, for those who would appreciate a synopsis of the events which lead to the formation of the Liverpool group, the seed of the partnership that would rock the entertainment world was sown in 1957 when John Winston Lennon met James Paul McCartney at a local school fete. As it happened, Lennon was appearing there with his own skiffle group - The Quarry Men. Other members joined the group and departed, but in 1958 they were joined by George Harrison, and later by Stuart Sutcliffe for a short period. In 1959 they became The Silver Beatles and when Pete Best joined them in 1960, they were retitled The Beatles. In 1961 they came to the attention of Brian Epstein who became their manager. He secured a recording contract with EMI which brought them into contact with producer George Martin. In the following year Pete Best was replaced by Ringo Starr (Richard Starkey), and the rest, of course, is history.

North Staffordshire fared exceedingly well in 1963 in so far as appearances of the Beatles were concerned. In the previous October, their debut single 'Love Me Do' had entered the top 50 sales chart within two days of release, and the group played at the Kings Hall, Stoke on 26th January 1963. Likewise, their second single 'Please, Please Me' hit No.1 in the NME chart in February after a rapid climb, and the group were on stage at Hanley's Gaumont Cinema on 3rd March. The Beatles subsequently paid return visits to the Kings Hall and the Gaumont on 19th April and 19th May respectively. By now the group was experiencing a fast growing popularity with clamorous scenes at their engagements. Sales of Beatles inspired merchandise were also gathering momentum and locally, in the *Sentinel*, outfitters Haydens were advertising Lybro jeans, as worn by the Beatles, from 24/6d! In the meantime, their next singles 'From Me To You' and 'She Loves You' enjoyed equal success, and after a busy schedule of summer shows and recording sessions, the Beatles performed at Trentham Gardens on Friday 11th October.

On the following day the *Sentinel* reported on the *'teenage hysteria'* which had hit Trentham on the previous evening. According to the newspaper *'three teenage girls had to be taken to hospital, and dozens of others given first aid by Red Cross attendants after some of the 3,000 crowd attempted to storm the stage.'* The venue's entertainments manager, the late Les Johnson, is reported as saying *'I've seen nothing like it - if I'd had enough tickets, I could have filled Stoke City football ground!'* Before the concert, two members of Trentham's staff had been working full time for two weeks, returning money to unsuccessful ticket applicants. The police description of the event was *'phenomenal'* after trying to cope with *'the largest, rowdiest crowd ever seen in the ballroom.'*   Some fans had travelled from as far away as Devon, and coachloads arrived from Liverpool and Birmingham. In the meantime, touts outside the main entrance were said to be selling the 7/6d tickets for £5.

On arrival at Trentham, the Beatles were *'escorted into the building by police who hurried them through a special entrance a few minutes before they took to the stage'.* Police dogs were also in attendance outside their dressing room which was padlocked. After their gig, reported by the *Sentinel* as lasting 30 minutes, members of the group dressed in their grey-brown collarless suits told the reporter that the crowd had given them *'the most enthusiastic welcome they had ever received!'* However, many fans must have been disappointed as a 2ft high pile of autograph books which had been placed outside the dressing room, were left unsigned.

One of Trentham's popular resident bands, the Ken Jones Orchestra, supported the Beatles on their visit to the ballroom. Ken had not heard of them, but his son told him that the Beatles *'were going to be it!'* and he was, of course, proved to be correct. He says that he *'will never forget the noise that went up - they nearly lifted the roof off!'* The veteran bandleader and composer contends that one could not compare his own musicians, who were all musically trained, to the Beatles. Nevertheless, he thought that John and Paul *'had a raw talent for writing that type of material which hit the pulse of the public at that time.'* After the performance, Ringo's drum kit remained on stage and a girl from the audience asked Ken if she could touch the drumsticks so, rightly or wrongly, he presented them to her. When he informed Ringo, he replied in his Liverpudlian accent - *'don't worry, I have a case full, fans are always requesting them as souvenirs!'* Ken says the Beatles only played for 20 minutes, and so to continue the dance programme which was scheduled to conclude at 1pm., the orchestra played mostly party and barn dance music and the fans entered into the atmosphere of the occasion and appeared to enjoy it. After the Beatles session, Ken recalls having his photograph taken with Paul McCartney, but to this day he has not seen a copy and is uncertain who the photographer was.[1]

Another witness to this momentous occasion was saxophonist Percy Le Rolland. Appearing with Ken Jones that evening, he and his colleagues should have initially played until 9pm., when the Beatles were due on stage. However, the group was late in arriving and, as a consequence, the orchestra had to carry on playing until they appeared at 9.20pm. According to Percy *'this was not popular with fellow band members as valuable drinking time was being lost at the nearby Bulls Head public house!'* He also agreed that once on stage the Beatles only played for 20 minutes. Personally, he thought John, Paul, George and Ringo *'a rough lot, none of them having the musical expertise of the Ken Jones sidemen.'* Having only played for such a short time, Percy thought that some of the fans were disappointed and afterwards, in the absence of the full band, he says that Ken Jones appeared somewhat perplexed, but attempted to carry on, as normal, with the youngsters experimenting with the various dances.[2]

Also in attendance at Trentham that evening was Graham Plimbley with the North

Staffordshire Hospital Broadcasting Unit. He recalled that *'it was total chaos that night - we ourselves had difficulty in gaining access.'* It had been arranged earlier for the Beatles to be interviewed after their performance, and they eventually arrived in the temporary studio. They immediately *'commenced fooling around, passing the microphone to one another, giving the impression that they were not taking the interview seriously, and that they just didn't want to know.'* Graham believes this was perhaps because to them the interviews were being conducted by the Hospital Broadcasts and not, say, one of the major radio stations. On attempting to commence the interview, John Lennon twice asked if they could *'use the 'f' word'* and at this Head of Programmes David Gredington concluded the recording. *'It was a complete disaster'* added Graham, and of course a unique opportunity to obtain a local recording was lost.[3] It is also perhaps worth noting that Barney Bamford was on hand with the hospital's mobile broadcasting unit. At the peak of his career, the Silverdale born broadcaster was seen everyday on the BBC Midlands Today programme.

The next day saw the Beatles rehearsing for the following evening's performance of Val Parnell's Sunday Night at the London Palladium. Starring Brook Benton and Des O'Connor, the programme was fully networked by ITV from the prestigious theatre and seen by 15 million viewers at peak time. The event was also covered by the late evening ITN news which had cameras in the group's theatre dressing room. It was a remarkable appearance at the so called *'home of the stars'* with screaming fans not only inside the theatre but in the street outside. Next day, Monday 14th October, a journalist chronicling the mayhem concocted the word 'Beatlemania' - a term that remains in use today. On the following Thursday, less than a week after playing at Trentham, the Beatles recorded I Want to Hold Your Hand at Abbey Road Studios, a track that was to become their first Christmas No.1, with advance sales of over 1 million. Those local fans who were present at Trentham that night in October 1963 were privileged to have witnessed a performance by the group at a unique time in their historic rise to super stardom. Few who were at the event are likely to forget the experience.

According to respected Beatles expert Garry Marsh, *'the Beatles were literally on the crest of the wave at Trentham, and they remain one of the best examples of what is now the hottest topic in the music industry - heritage rock.'*[4] Their image and music continues to illustrate not only the 1960s, but also the latter half of the 20th Century, and they have left us possibly the greatest legacy of popular music ever recorded.

NOTES

1. Telephone interview with author 24th February 2003.
2. Telephone interview with author 24th February 2003.
3. Interview with author 11th November 2003.
4. Telephone interview with author 6th March 2003.

John Broome CBE at Trentham in the early 1980s. *Courtesy Philip Bradbeer*

Repairing Trentham Lake following subsidence damage. Photo by author 1986.

22. 'PROJECT TRENTHAM'

By the late 1970s, the cost of maintaining the former 'Potteries playground' had risen inexorably. Investment in new amenities had ceased, and some buildings were in an advanced state of decay, with maintenance having fallen to a minimum. The famous gardens were a mere shadow of their former glory. By October 1981, the number of staff had fallen from a peak of 140 to 35.[1]

It was obvious that if the historic estate was to be saved, the situation could not be allowed to continue. As it happened, the 'saviour' turned out to be the entrepeneur John Broome, who had transformed nearby Alton Towers into a highly successful theme park. On purchasing Trentham Gardens on 30th September 1981, he immediately set about restoring the buildings and began an extensive replanting programme.[2] To achieve this, 160 were employed, together with casual staff, plus outside contractors for specific tasks. Within a short period, approximately £0.5m had been committed by Broome's company to arresting and reversing the long, 'sad decline' of the estate.[3] However, he also had further plans. After a six month research study, he revealed his vision for the creation at Trentham of *'a complete inland sports, leisure and conference resort'* involving *'a complex of facilities of a kind not seen in Britain before.'* It was, as one former employee quipped admiringly - *'certainly a case of new broom sweeping clean!'*

The ambitious proposals were published in a consultation portfolio under the title 'Project Trentham' with a foreword written by Broome himself in his capacity as Chairman of the newly formed Trentham Gardens Ltd. In this he explained that, whilst the proposed recreation facilities would be *'invaluable and substantial',* they would not be the primary way in which the project would serve the community. *'The main benefits'* he wrote, *'would be the employment and the wealth generated for the local economy.'* Approximately 1,500 jobs were envisaged, with annual income from visitors then estimated at £10m. Also included in the far-reaching proposals was the preservation of the landscape and historic buildings, with a viable use being provided for them. In conclusion, however, Broome stressed that all this *'had to be paid for'* and that whilst the different parts of the scheme were *'interdependent and part of a single financial structure',* the omission of any part, particularly that involving the raising of capital, would *'throw out of balance'* the whole project.[4]

It was envisaged that the proposals contained in the 'Trentham Project' would be *'sympathetically'* carried out, subject to planning permission, in phases over a three year period, with a particular regard for *'the character of the estate'* and those parts designated as a Special Landscape Area and/or a Site of Special Scientific Interest. It was, however, also emphasised that the proposals could be affected by a possible M6/A50 link road which would slice through part of Monument Hill.

Phase I included provision of the all important access arrangements. To avoid congestion on local roads, improved access was proposed off a new roundabout at the junction of the A34 Stone Road/A5035 Longton Road. Inside the complex, extensive parking and servicing facilities were planned off a new access road, and a tramcar for those who wished to be conveyed from the car parks to the admission booths. Once inside, whilst the grounds and gardens would be generally pedestrianised, a *'people moving system'* would link different parts. In the meantime, a German built land train had been brought in to transport visitors around the estate. Former general manager Philip Bradbeer remembers it as *'a fine piece of engineering with five coaches, and so easy to drive.'*

With the 1.5 mile lake central to Trentham, various water based activities were planned including rowing boats, 'quiet' miniature Mississippi style stern-wheelers, fishing, and a floating restaurant. Also incorporated in this phase was the retention of the open air swimming pool. This was to be completely refurbished and updated with features such as a wave machine and long twisting water slides. Provision of a gymnasium, jacuzzi, sauna, solarium, bar and restaurant were also planned for the existing pool buildings. Yet a further restaurant *'of high quality'* was proposed for the surviving west entrance conservatory of the former hall. The exterior was to be *'sympathetically preserved'* as part of the rejuvenation work, and it was considered that the proposal would provide *'a harmonious viable use'* for the important listed building.

The extensive portfolio also detailed proposals for a major scheme of floodlighting for the trees, gardens, river, buildings and fountains which would become *'the largest computerised playing fountains in the world!'* Refurbishment of the bandstand featured in the work, together with upgrading of the partly derelict fairground to a children's *'adventureland'.*

Not surprisingly, proposals relating to the famous ballroom were of particular interest to many. Briefly, the intention was that it be *'extensively refurbished'* and fitted with the most modern equipment for entertainment, conferences, exhibitions etc. In turn, the ballroom would form the basis of a Trentham Centre, the existing floorspace being substantially extended by approximately 18,000sq.ft to the rear, with the transfer of a renovated exhibition hall from the Italian Gardens. Subsequently, a high quality 150 bedroom hotel would be added to the centre, being separated by natural screening and garden from any traffic. At a later stage, a further 200 bedroom low rise hotel and sports club was to be provided on an area to the west of the lake. Sporting facilities were to include floodlit tennis courts, riding trails, golf and equestrian event courses. A prime aim was that Trentham would become a sporting *'centre of excellence'.*

For the many daytime visitors anticipated, and also staying tourists, a major new feature was proposed in the form of an Italian village. To achieve this, the intention was to make *'harmonious use'* of the Italianate styled laundry houses and stable block off Park Drive, which were described as being in *'a poor structural state'.* Craft shops, a restaurant, a tea shop and a country life museum would occupy ground floor level with holiday apartments on the first floor. Continuing the Italian theme, the nearby southerly stable block would be formed into a main square or piazza, with craft workshops etc in the surrounding existing buildings.

In a move to secure essential capital for the whole scheme, and to provide much needed housing accommodation in the area at that time, restoration was proposed of a number of the estate's existing dilapidated houses, some of which were listed. In other 'unused' areas, a number of *'small estates of high quality, low density'* dwellings were proposed. Linked to the sporting facilities, clusters of high quality lodges would provide self-catering accommodation. It was envisaged that some of the properties would become second homes or timeshare, whilst a number would also be needed to house estate employees who would be required to work unsociable hours. Being linked with Alton Towers (then without a hotel) it was considered that both venues would benefit from the provision of accommodation for visitors, especially those from overseas.

The proposals were formally submitted to Stafford Borough Council on 15th July 1982. A number of minor amendments were received, following which outline planning permission was finally granted on 23rd November 1982, subject to numerous conditions[5]. However, with the exception of the access arrangements and the provision of the new roundabout at the junction of the A34 Stone Road/A5035 Longton Road, the planning permission was never implemented. In the meantime, it became evident that there was increased subsidence damage from mining activity. A number of properties were demolished in the Trentham area and at an earlier planning inquiry into proposals to convert nearby Barlaston Hall into apartments, a National Coal Board official *'expressed concern that foundations were secure to prepare it for further mining work in the area'.*[6]

At Trentham Gardens there was evidence of serious damage to the lake which eventually resulted in it being drained for a lengthy period to enable repairs to be carried out. Water Authority officials rescued some 40,000 fish in a *'dramatic race against time'*. Whilst thousands did not survive, 2 tonnes of bream, roach, perch, tench and carp were netted and transferred to the River Trent and Trent & Mersey Canal.[7] The abandoned open air swimming pool was demolished during this period.

By this time, however, Trentham Gardens had again changed ownership. In 1984, John Broome's company sold the 770 acre estate to the National Coal Board.[8] Whether or not the sole reasoning behind the sale was the problems relating to mining activity is difficult to determine. An official of the local planning authority also pointed out that Broome's proposals for the properties at the northern end of the estate (the laundry houses, etc) were not implemented because they were subsequently sold and converted into luxury apartments.

Opinion on the Broome era at Trentham remains divided. There are those who consider that John Broome was a *'man of great vision'* and that, whilst he may have had a few setbacks in his lifetime, nevertheless the legacy of what he achieved at Alton Towers is there to see. One assumes that his Trentham Gardens would have achieved a similar status but on a different scale and style - and the ballroom and open air swimming pool would have remained popular attractions. On the other hand, some remain unforgiving about the alleged unauthorised removal of certain 'treasures' during the period.

NOTES

1. John L. Broome *Project Trentham* (undated) Foreword p1.
2. Conveyance from Countess of Sutherland to Trentham Gardens Ltd (Land Registry).
3. John L. Broome op.cit.   4. Ibid.
5. Stafford Borough Council reference N13607.
6. *Stafford Newsletter* 9th October 1981
7. *Sentinel* (undated)
8. Conveyance dated 12th April 1984 (Land Registry)

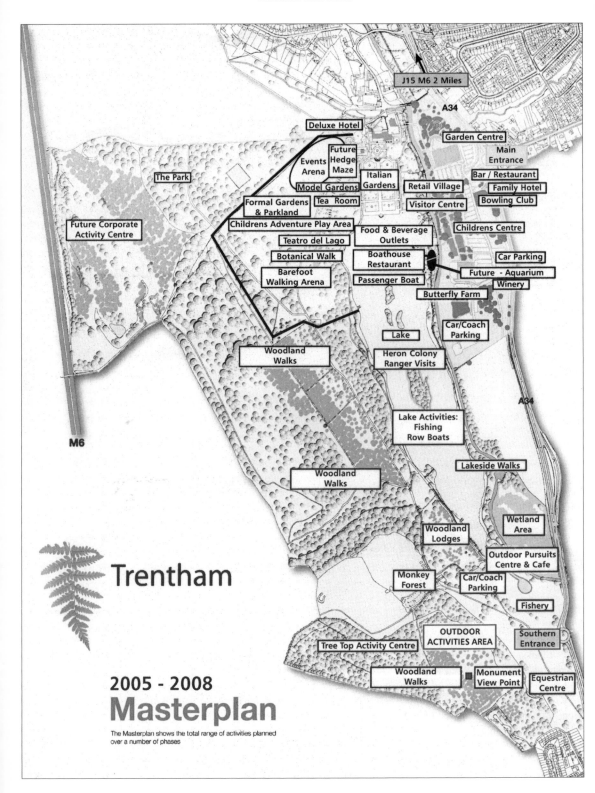

J15 M6 2 Miles

A34

Deluxe Hotel
Garden Centre
Main Entrance
Future Hedge Maze
Events Arena
The Park
Italian Gardens
Bar / Restaurant
Model Gardens
Retail Village
Family Hotel
Formal Gardens & Parkland
Tea Room
Visitor Centre
Bowling Club
Childrens Adventure Play Area
Childrens Centre
Future Corporate Activity Centre
Food & Beverage Outlets
Teatro del Lago
Botanical Walk
Boathouse Restaurant
Car Parking
Barefoot Walking Arena
Passenger Boat
Future - Aquarium
Winery
Butterfly Farm
Car/Coach Parking
Lake
Woodland Walks
Heron Colony Ranger Visits

A34

Lake Activities: Fishing Row Boats

M6

Woodland Walks

Lakeside Walks

Wetland Area

Woodland Lodges

Outdoor Pursuits Centre & Cafe

Monkey Forest
Car/Coach Parking

Trentham

Fishery

Tree Top Activity Centre
OUTDOOR ACTIVITIES AREA
Southern Entrance

2005 - 2008
Masterplan

The Masterplan shows the total range of activities planned
over a number of phases

Woodland Walks
Monument View Point
Equestrian Centre

Courtesy Trentham Leisure.

23. THE GREAT PHOENIX RISES FROM THE ASHES

The Trentham ballroom in the 1940s..

On 24th September 1996, ownership of the Trentham Gardens estate was to change yet again.[1] On this occasion the purchaser was Trentham Leisure Ltd, a joint venture between the Birmingham property company St. Modwen Properties plc., and the German entrepeneur Willi Reitz. More or less immediately, the company embarked on a planning consultation exercise with the local authorities concerned, English Heritage and other interested parties before submitting an application to Stafford Borough Council for leisure and retail development. A lengthy public inquiry followed before outline planning permission was finally granted by the Secretary of State on 12th November 2001.[2]

In 2003, after seven years of detailed research and planning, the company unveiled plans for the first phase of a £100m restoration and revamp of Trentham Gardens.[3] Briefly, the wholesale refurbishment included the re-creation of Sir Charles Barry's famous gardens (although not precisely, as some of the plants no longer exist!) with leading garden designers Tom Stuart-Smith and Peit Oudolf involved in the intricate task of restoration, as well as introducing contemporary landscape features.

The first phase was completed and the site officially re-opened on 29th May 2004 by the late Sir Stanley Clarke CBE, then Chairman of St. Modwen Developments Ltd. At that ceremony his wife, Lady Hilda Clarke, unveiled the restored statue of Perseus which has proudly stood at the head of the lake since the 19th Century. One of the largest freestanding bronze sculptures in the country, it was commissioned by the 2nd Duke of Sutherland at the time of the reconstruction of Trentham Hall in 1840. The statue is a high quality copy of Cellini's 16th Century masterpiece which stands at the Loggia Del Lanzi in Florence. The plinth was rebuilt, and the original lakeside landing reconstructed of Terne Hollington sandstone from a re-opened seam at the famous quarry near Cheadle. A further 176

Gardener Heather McFall with a few of the thousands of plants used to restore Trentham's Italian Garden.
Below: bulb planting. Taken by author 2004.

The gardens today with their new planting.
The parish church and the remains of Trentham Hall are seen in the background. *Courtesy Trentham Leisure.*

Visitors heading for a little retail therapy in the Retail Village. *Courtesy Trentham Leisure.*

tonnes were used to restore crumbling balustrades and other important stone features on the estate. Stone from Hollington was originally used in the mid 19th Century for such items within the gardens.

Since the official re-opening, access to the restored gardens is by a new visitor centre, linked to car parks via a new bridge over the River Trent. However, the public have free access to the woodland and lakeside areas. Also, a new major garden centre operated by the Blue Diamond Company of Guernsey has opened and this is the centrepiece of a retail village, the first phase comprising 20 lifestyle, heritage, leisure, craft and restaurant units. In December 2004, it was reported that 300 were employed at Trentham, and the figure was to double by the end of 2005. It was envisaged that more than 1,000 would be employed as the development progressed.[4]

In the past, visitors to Trentham Gardens took trips on the lake and this popular tradition is being revived thanks to a specially commissioned £150,000 electrically driven catamaran. The 42 seater will make trips daily and be available for private hire in the evenings. At the time of writing, it is understood that the vessel will dock at either end of the lake to enable passengers to undertake a round trip, or disembark at one end to walk back along the lakeside or through the woodland. The vessel was commissioned to be ecologically-friendly, so as not to disturb the wildlife or fishermen.

A second phase of development lasting around two years is presently in progress, the most ambitious aspect of which involves the reconstruction of Trentham Hall into a 5 star luxury hotel. Other planned developments include a floating stage for concerts and drama productions ('Teatro Del Lago' - the theatre on the lake), a winery, a gardening academy, an outdoor activity centre, holiday lodges, a fishing centre and a further phase of the retail village.

Restoration of the gardens and parkland will continue through 2005/6 as part of the overall project to create one of Europe's leading visitor destinations at Trentham. Wildlife is a vital element of the estate with the proposed development featuring a long-term commitment to nature conservation. Trentham is notable, of course, for its historic herd of fallow deer, but also boasts one of the largest heronries in the country. At the last count there were 42 breeding pairs based on an island on the lake. Restoration of the parkland and woodland has provided an improved environment for birds and it is not unusual to see kingfishers in the area.

Late last year I had the privilege of seeing the planting at Trentham in progress. Accompanied by

An artist takes advantage of the Lake in 2004.
Photo by author

gardener Heather McFall, I was informed that the beds were being prepared for some 70,000 plants which had already been delivered on site. Only by witnessing this, can one appreciate the enormity of the task in hand. The list of plants seemed endless, from asters to verbena. In another part of the gardens, in what appeared a small bed, 2,000 bulbs were being planted!

Meanwhile, as a secondary entrance to the venue is being constructed to the south at Strongford, the towering statue of the Duke looks down on all he surveys. I would like to think that he approves...

NOTES

1. Conveyance (Land Registry).
2. Decision letter from the Government Office for the West Midlands.
3. The *Sentinel* 12th December 2003 & *The Guardian* 7th August 2003.
4. The *Sentinel* 28th December 2004.

The Duke looks down on all he surveys....
Chantrey's colossal statue of the 1st Duke of Sutherland which
dominates Monument Hill at the southern end of Trentham Lake.
Photograph by author 2004.

TWO VIEWS OF THE
LAKE
IN THE 1970S.

VIEW OF TRENTHAM GARDENS.
LAKE & WOODS.

The refurbished gardens looking north towards the parish church and the former Sculpture Garden with its clock tower. *Courtesy Trentham Leisure.*

The refurbished Italian Gardens looking towards the lake and Monument Hill. *Courtesy Trentham Leisure.*

POSTSCRIPT: POSTCARDS OF OLD TRENTHAM

Postcards from Mrs Barbara Hobson and the Bebbington collection